The Changing Face
of Clifton

Van Wilson

Published by York Archaeological Trust 2011
47 Aldwark, York YO1 7BX
www.yorkarchaeology.co.uk

Designed and typeset by Snowgoose Promotions
Cover design by Snowgoose Promotions

Printed by
Zebra Print Management

ISBN No. 978-1-874454-55-7

Front cover: *Homestead Park donkey rides 1904 (Joseph Rowntree Foundation)*

Back cover: *The Ouse at Clifton c1900*

CONTENTS

FOREWORD

I remember my first day at St. Peter's School, vividly. I had moved to the school in the summer term from Leeds Grammar School when my father became manager of Boots the Chemist in Coney Street. I was a fanatical Leeds United fan. Saturday school was not something I had experienced before. On this Saturday Leeds United were playing Liverpool in the final of the FA Cup. Hardly the best start for me at St. Peter's.

To make matters worse, the fag system was still in use and I was assigned to the Head of House. The fag would go on errands for the senior boys... sweets, books, just about anything. As kick off approached I settled to watch the match on television. Then came the call. Would I go to the shop and get half a dozen things so that the seniors could watch the match? I was outraged! Told him to go and get the things himself and received my first discipline card, a whole page which started... "Discipline is the means whereby we are trained in orderliness, good conduct and the habit of getting the best out of oneself..."

I have to say, though, that my time at St. Peter's was fabulous and my love of Clifton was really established then. I am excited about the book. I wish

you all the best of luck. The school is still central to the vibrancy of the place, but there's much more isn't there? Enjoy!

Harry Gration

ACKNOWLEDGEMENTS

This book could not have been written without the help and support of a number of people. I would like to thank the following organisations who have given financial support to this project –

RM Burton Charitable Trust, Friends of York Archaeological Trust, Sheldon Memorial Trust, Patricia and Donald Shepherd Charitable Trust, the Yorkshire Architectural and York Archaeological Society, York Common Good Trust and Yorkshire Philosophical Society.fo

I wish to thank the following who allowed me to copy photographs -

Neal Guppy, Janet McCullough of the Joseph Rowntree Foundation, The Press in York, Eileen Race, Father Ross Thompson of St Joseph's Church, Kath Webb and staff of the Borthwick Institute for Archives, Jessica Willis, York Oral History Society and Yorkshire Air Museum.

Many thanks to Oliver Bostock and Christine Kyriacou for taking photographs for the book.

Thanks are due to the following for help with queries –

George Briffa, General Manager of The Grange Hotel, The staff of Haverford - the York Youth Hostel, Philip Johnson, the late Jennifer Kaner, Kara of The Gent's Barbers at Clifton Green, Ivan Martin, Hugh Murray, David Poole, the staff of York Explore and Joel Kerry, local studies librarian, for allowing me to use the photographs of the Ogle family and the memories of William Dowell which are deposited in the library.

I would like to thank Harry Gration for his foreword to this publication and I am particularly grateful to Mike Race for help with research and for taking and copying many of the photographs.

I would particularly like to thank those who shared their stories and photographs with me –

Joan Aherne, Charles Alcorn, Margaret Arnold, Nick Banks, Gerald Barker, Rosanne Bostock, Colin Carr, Margaret Chapman, Keith Cowl, Peter Dale, Derrick Dandy, Peter Dench, Sheila Goater, Richard Harwood, Doug Heald, Roy Hodgson, Guy Jefferson, Henry King, Eliza Kirby, John Linfoot, Malcolm Maher, Gill May, Derek Metcalfe, Lena Mills, Mary Morris, Hugh Murray, Marilyn Powell, Jeremy Prendergast, Jonathan Prendergast, Eleanor R, Bill Sessions, Anthony Skeels, Carole Smith, Lucy Staples, Marion Tweedy, Peter Willow, Pauline Wright, Pam Young.

From York Archaeological Trust I must thank Chief Executive John Walker and Director of Attractions Sarah Maltby for their support. Grateful thanks to Mike Andrews for scanning numerous photographs and to Gordon Webber for his design of the publication. In particular, I wish to thank the Trust Archivist Christine Kyriacou for excellent fund-raising, project management and editing.

Chapter 1

EARLY CLIFTON

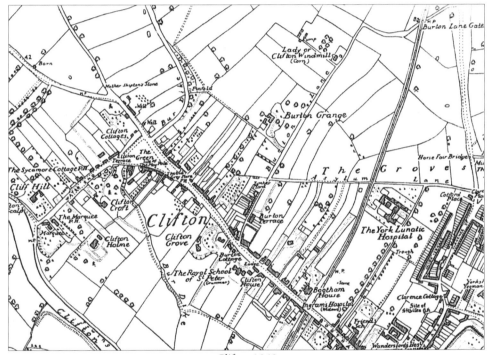

Clifton 1849

In the Domesday Book of 1086, a survey of assets ordered by William the Conqueror, land in Clifton was owned by St Peter's School, Count Alan of Richmond, the Archbishop and Canons of York Minster. There were 18 carucates of land, and 50 acres of meadow. A carucate was the amount of land tillable by a team of eight oxen in a ploughing season. The township fell into three manors – Clifton, Strensall, and Acomb with

1

Holgate and Clifton. In 1088, Lordship of the Manors of Clifton and Overton was granted by King William II to St Mary's Abbey. An Award between the Abbot and the Mayor and Commonalty of York, concerning the bounds of common and pasture land, indicates the custom of special tenure of land by particular individuals during the time of growing hay and corn from sowing to reaping, and of common tenure by all citizens for pasturage during the remainder of the year. Clifton remained in the ownership of the Abbey until Henry VIII dissolved the monasteries in 1536 and all land passed to the Crown.

The name of Clifton, like that of nearby Rawcliffe, was derived from the cliff or scope at the Ings, near the present Clifton Bridge. Water End, the road from Clifton Green to the Bridge, was an important area in the late 13th century. The Cistercians of Byland Abbey had property on the site that is now the Homestead and Haverford, the youth hostel. In addition to its assize court where mostly petty crimes were heard, it was also the abbey's shipping point for exporting wool along the Ouse to Flemish and Italian merchants. Byland Abbey delivered 203 sacks of wool between 1299 and 1305. Fountains Abbey sent 130 sacks between 1279 and 1284. Fountains Abbey also had a town house in Clifton for officials engaged in the business. A sack was thought to contain the wool of between 250 and 300 sheep.

In the 1530s, the Ingleby family were tenants of much of Clifton. In 1560, most of Clifton was bought by York merchant William Robinson, Lord Mayor in 1581 and 1594, who also acquired the Manor of Rawcliffe in 1582, the Manor of Clifton in 1600 and the rectory of St Olave's in 1613 with part of its tithes, (the rest bought by his son in 1622). In a survey of the 37 properties belonging to the Robinsons in 1605, the amount of land with each property varied from three acres to 18 perches.

The Freemen of Bootham Stray from ancient times enjoyed the rights of pasturage over Clifton Moor. Because of this, it was necessary to have a formal Enclosure Award in 1763, when 91 acres were awarded to the Mayor and Commonalty to be held in trust, and 21½ acres allotted to make a road for the passage of cattle. Eight acres were assigned as public highway. The fields and closes from Clifton up to Skelton included Hobthrush Beds, Ashtree Close, Ingends Close, Lusteran Carr, Reed Lands, Wad Garth, Unthank and Bull Butt. Ownership passed down through the Robinson family. William's grandson, Sir William Robinson, Sheriff of York in 1639, who lived at Newby Hall near Ripon, bought more land in Clifton in 1637 and 1642. Sir William's grandson, also Sir William Robinson, was Lord Mayor in 1700, and MP for York from 1697 to 1722. Clifton was very much a farming area with a number of small dairy farms and market gardens, smallholdings, garths and crofts. In 1766, Clifton got its own workhouse governed by Thomas Simpson and his wife, with a committee for the management of the poor.

It was Sir William's grandson, Thomas Philip Robinson, who became third Baron Grantham and then second Earl de Grey in 1833. He was a Privy Counsellor, first Lord of the Admiralty and a Knight of the Garter. He was also Colonel of the Yorkshire Hussar regiment of cavalry and later Lord Lieutenant of Ireland.

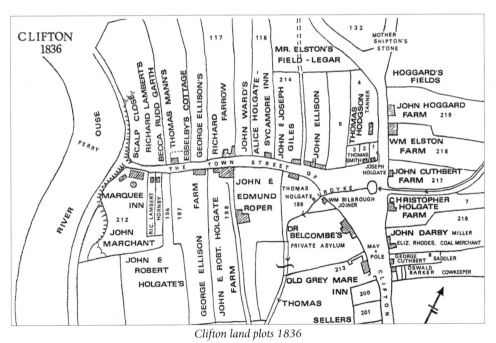

Clifton land plots 1836

3

In 1836 Earl de Grey auctioned off much of his land in Clifton, Rawcliffe and Skelton. Clifton was still a village in 1836, with only 700 residents, considered by York people as a 'place for healthful recreation'. The main road was a turnpike 'made up with stone dumped in the ruts and potholes and levelled off by wheels of passing wagons'. But soon the development began in earnest as lots were gradually sold. Gas first came to Clifton in the same decade. The bill for the township in 1839 was £12.10s. Most of the big houses were the first to be lit, such as Clifton Croft, Dr Belcombe's Asylum and Bootham Hospital. The 1839 rate books show 52 owners of property in Clifton, of which eight were women (usually widows of owners). Several builders had bought garths and closes, and developed terraces or crescents, named after themselves, such as (Oswald) Barker's Terrace. Earl De Grey still retained 45 properties, with Seth Agar, a city councillor, obtaining much of the land north of Clifton Green. In 1848, 700 acres of land in the Manor of Rawcliffe was also sold. In 1886 the York city boundary was extended to include part of Clifton, although there had been some initial resistance. The Robinson - De Grey family and its heirs remained Lord of the Manor of Clifton, until 1919 when the title was sold, with Rawcliffe, to York Corporation by Mary Evelyn Compton-Vyner and Violet Aline, great grand-daughters of Thomas Robinson, Earl de Grey. Their father Robert Charles De Grey Vyner, who died in 1915, had owned Fairfield Manor (see chapter on Doctors and Hospitals).

BEATING THE BOUNDS

Beating the Bounds was an ancient ceremony where the minister and churchwardens would 'perambulate' the boundaries of the parish on Rogation Sunday, the fifth Sunday after Easter. This was both to lay claim to the boundaries, before maps were easily available, and also to ask God to bless the crops and the farmers (rogare in Latin means 'to ask'), with the singing of hymns. As part of the ceremony, a group of boys, armed with sticks of birch or willow, beat the boundary markers, usually trees. Often the boys themselves would be whipped if they did not remember the exact lines of the boundary, and if groups from more than one parish took part, fighting was the result. George Benson in his book on York in 1911, describes the ceremony in Clifton.

St Michael le Belfrey parish had 19 detached portions, their boys mustered with sticks and stones at the Minster west end, whilst boys of St Olave's gathered outside Bootham Bar. Above a hundred were ranged on each side, and after throwing a few stones, they rushed to hold the bar. Ugly blows were dealt and even after Belfreyites were victorious, some Olavites hidden in Manor Yard caught them in the rear and gave them a sound thrashing. Prayers were said... after which stay laces for women and boot laces for men were given out and armfuls taken to distribute on the way, and boundaries were chalked. Beer and cakes were partaken of on Clifton Green.

Beyond Burdike the boundary between St Olave's and the Belfrey continued into the centre of the river, and a shilling was given to the boy who dived into the Ouse with the chalk in his mouth, and put a mark on the post.

MANOR COURT LEET

Manors existed in Anglo Saxon times, but after the Norman Conquest, the term meant 'an estate organised under aristocratic administration'. The Manor had a Lord with his own lands, and tenants who had holdings and rights of common. The Manor Court was set up to impose penalties on anyone found guilty of damaging or neglecting property on the Manor lands. There were several thousand active courts in the 18th century. Today only 21 survive, six of which are in Yorkshire, with one in Clifton. The Court was no respecter of persons. Seebohm Rowntree of the Homestead and a general from the White House were fined, with Clifton airfield and later the RAF being fined for not keeping ditches clean.

The Court Leet is the annual sitting of the jury. Anthony Skeels is a juror of the Clifton Manor Court Leet.

The records are headed the 'Court Leet and Frankpledge' with the Court Baron of the Lord of the Manor. Not every court leet is a 'court leet with a view of frankpledge'. Ours is a pretty significant one. The view of frankpledge regulates the working of tithings. If they had grazing rights on the Ings or rights for cutting hay, the Court Leet

Manor Court Leet meeting at Old Grey Mare 2007. L to R – Patrick Malham, Anne Platt, Anthony Skeels, Elizabeth Ellis, Carol Martin, Derek Bellerby, Jennie Skeels, Dr Julian Bedford, Dr Peter Dench. Front - Ivan Martin (Anthony Skeels)

would say how much of that they could have, how much would be tithed and where it would go.

The court has been held every year since the 12th century. On the second Wednesday in October, we have a meeting where we're all summoned. [It was held at the Burton Stone Inn after 1945, then at the Old Grey Mare. It is now held in the Mansion House with the Sheriff of York in attendance]. *If members of the court leet don't turn up, they are fined. If they are late, they are fined. In days gone by it would have been a legal summons. On the door of wherever the court is held, there is a summons pinned to the outside. In the old days it would have been nailed.*

The principal items are the records of the Court Leet and the Court Baron, the first dealing with petty crimes, manorial appointments, the second with land transfer. The two courts are dealt with at

Manor Court Leet meeting at the Mansion House 2010. Back L to R –
Anthony Skeels, Foreman of Jury, David Robinson, Dr Alan Scott, Dr Peter Dench, Jennie Skeels,
Ivan Martin. Front L to R – Dr Julian Bedford, Anne Platt, Sheriff Richard Watson, Derek
Bellerby, Bailiff (Anthony Skeels)

one sitting and the records are noted in the same document. It
was originally in rolls, later in volumes, and the records, with the
exception of the Commonwealth period, are in Latin, until 1734.
Separate from these would be rentals and also a customal which
recites the customs, rights and obligations of the Manor. The Lord
may also have a plan and terrier of his immense lands.

Ten jurymen and a foreman are sworn in. Then they make the request
for a sheriff, two byelaw men, and two affearers. We are then sent
out to 'diligently look and find that everything is all right'. Some
places have ale tasters. I don't know why they didn't have ale tasters
here, such a pity! In Easingwold they had two constables, four water
sewer men and a Pinder. [Pinders were the officers who collected
fines from owners who let animals stray or graze without common
rights. The 'pinfold' was used to pen the animals in overnight].

At six o'clock, we're called back, the reports are read and the court is closed till the following year. We have a meal, we pay for that, in the old days the Lord of the Manor would have paid for that. But the Sheriff's office pays for the wine. In 2010 the proceedings were presided over by the Sheriff of York, Councillor Richard Watson. Certain residents were sworn in as bye-law men, Alan Scott, Peter Dench and Ivan Martin. They were 'charged with conducting the duties of the Court, namely to visit and inspect specified watercourse within the Manor of Clifton and report without fear or favour, any nuisances, malfunction or any other irregularity to the Bailiff before nightfall of that day'.

The Court Leet was almost working like an overseer to make sure the tenants kept their land tidy, clean and gave the correct tithing. The fact that we probably never collect the money from the fines is no matter, we still set them. The watercourses, now they are looked after by Yorkshire Water, it used to be the Upper Kyle and Ouse Drainage Board.

Two or three years ago we found an awful lot of things. We made a suggestion that we located the area where it was worst and the council put a skip near the beck at that point. It's getting difficult now to get into the beck in certain places, things like brambles have grown. One regular thing is children putting planks across the beck to make bridges. Our job is to make sure that everything doesn't get blocked up. The reports would include such things as two discarded bicycles and a tubular chair below the water at the lakeside, a bicycle under the bridge, a large boulder in the beck and a number of discarded bricks.

Chapter 2

CLIFTON GREEN

Clifton Green c1900 (York Oral History Society)

Guide books describe Clifton Green as 'one of York's chief delights', and it is seen as a lovely oasis in the centre of the traffic laden streets of Clifton, Water End and Water Lane. Pam Young believes that,

> *Clifton Green is a special place. It's a pretty place, and the daffodils around it in spring are beautiful.*

Maria Husband lived at Clifton View near to Burton Stone Lane until her death in 1913. She was the daughter of Dr William Husband, Sheriff of York, and sister of Dr William Dalla Husband, who became Lord Mayor in 1858. Maria was known as a benefactress to various causes and in 1885 she helped to found the 'York Band of Mercy or Juvenile Society for the Promotion of Kindness to Animals'. One of her concerns was that cattle were being driven through Clifton towards the cattle market with nowhere to stop for a drink. She organised subscriptions, in 1883, to erect the horse and cattle drinking trough which still remains on the right side of the Green, replacing a small pond which had been declared insanitary. The pond is marked on the Ordnance Survey map of 1850 on the north corner of the Green and was fed by the Bur Dike which flowed along the north side of Water Lane and was culverted under the top end of Clifton. Eliza Kirby, who lived in Compton Street near the Green, recalls,

Horse trough (Van Wilson)

Miss Husband looked after the horse trough. She was a maiden lady and thought the world of animals. She engaged a man to clean the trough out once or twice a week. He'd go with a bucket and broom and empty it, sweep it out and she saw it was refilled. The horses coming in from Shipton Road, they didn't have to be told, they knew where it was, they used to pull up themselves, they'd always have a drink.

The cost of the trough was £130, and Miss Husband herself contributed £14. In 1983 it became a Grade II listed Horse Drinking Trough and Canopy. A sign above it reads 'The police are instructed to apprehend anyone playing with the drinking water'. Beneath the main trough is a lower one for dogs. Animals also came to the Green for the Clifton Feast and Maria Husband organised refreshment for the fairground workers when they visited the area.

The Clifton Feast took place long before the area was built up with houses. The Yorkshire Gazette of 7th May 1892 reported that, 'In accord with the custom of past generations, the Cliftonians held their annual feast on May Day, the first of the 'merrie month'. The village green was occupied by various stalls, swing boats, shooting galleries, and various commodities indispensable to make up the modern feast, and mirth and gaiety held predominant sway'.

The feast was traditionally a day off for farm labourers. Clifton Green originally had a Maypole on a slight mound (now covered by a tree), for the dancing of the May Queen and her followers with their coloured ribbons. May 1st is also the feast of St Philip and St James (as Clifton Parish Church is known), the patron saints of workers and a festival celebrating the fertility of springtime. In medieval times, the Lord of the Manor would invite his subjects to a feast in his honour.

Lady Ethel Thomson, daughter of the Honourable Reginald Parker and his wife Katherine, whose family lived at Clifton Lodge at the turn of the 20th century, recalled the Clifton Feast in her book 'Clifton Lodge', although she did not take part in the festivities.

An annual Fair was held on May Day or the nearest convenient Saturday, with fun booths and sideshows which we were not allowed to approach. We cast longing eyes on the attractions of the coconut shies, the shining metallic horses of a roundabout and the exciting looking young gypsies with red kerchiefs round their necks, with whom we were longing to talk.

Eliza Kirby remembers,

*You saved up for the Clifton Feast. If you could run an errand
for anybody you'd maybe get a penny. There were hurdy gurdies,
roundabouts and swingboats. I could manage the swingboats but
those roundabouts I didn't like. They went too fast and I got dizzy
going round and round. They had to work it by hand. You got so
many rounds for tuppence.*

Clifton Green shops just beyond Grey Mare pub c1905

In September 1904, prominent members of the Clifton community met
together at the Grey Mare to discuss the preservation of Clifton Green.
They included the chairman, Rev Charles Alexander, minister of St Philip
and St James Church opposite the Green, James Melrose of Clifton Croft,
pasture masters Thomas Milner and George Plummer (the dairyman
who lived at 'Highcliffe'), James Smith Law, landlord of the Grey Mare,
and Mr Lofthouse representing John Smith's Brewery. Arthur Hudson,

ecclesiastical lawyer, also attended, as did Ernest Dodsworth of St Peter's Grove, senior partner of Gray and Dodsworth solicitors and Sheriff of York, the Hon. Reginald Parker of Clifton Lodge and Wharton Watson, who lived at Fairfield on Shipton Road and later Clifton Terrace, the private secretary to Robert Charles De Grey Vyner for 30 years. Presumably women were not invited as Mr E Parker represented Mrs Nellie Farmery, who ran a servants' registry office and confectioners' near to Clifton Green.

The meeting was called because the Lords of the Manor, Earl Cowper and De Grey Vyner, felt that the Green was not properly protected and were concerned that 'encroachments and footpaths were taking place on the Green'. They suggested handing over the rights to the York Corporation, but the pasture masters and others wanted the control to remain in local hands. Reginald Parker, Arthur Hudson and the two pasture masters formed a committee to prepare a scheme for the Green's future. It was agreed that the only event to take place on the Green would be the two day feast in May. The profit from this (approximately £3) was paying for the maintenance of the Green. A Memorandum of Agreement was set up to manage and maintain the Green and the fencing. But this did not include the trees or the land itself. They decided that the fencing would be like a racecourse fence which cost 2s 6d a yard for 450 yards. A donation of 14 guineas had already been promised.

In 1919 the City Council became the Lord of the Manor of Clifton. Joan Aherne's family lived near the Green when she was born in 1932. Her grandparents owned three cottages,

Just past Clifton Dale. Eventually they sold two of them off and owned the one next to the guest houses.

When the fair came, that was lovely. I just watched it from inside. I maybe would go and get some toffee apples. It got dangerous when the roads got busy. It used to make a mess as well. All this rain, and when they went, getting those great big vans off, it churned it all up.

The Church newsletter reported that 'the travellers in charge of the vans and caravans at the May Day Feast on the Green were entertained in the schoolroom for breakfast'. But they also had to listen to a talk by a lady from the Travellers' Total Abstinence Association and the tone of the report about them is somewhat patronising! 'The behaviour and appearance of the guests showed a marked improvement of former years. The kindness shown in this way has a humanising effect'.

Joan felt that the Green was

A focal place. Lots of children in those days. From chapel [Clifton Methodist Church] *we'd go down on a Sunday evening in summer and have a little service and hymn singing on the Green. There's a circular wrought iron seat. We'd congregate round there and people would bring chairs out. And the Salvation Army band, particularly at Christmas, came on the Green and played.*

Iron seat at Clifton Green (Van Wilson)

The York and Ainsty Hunt sometimes met on the Green, as Roy Hodgson, whose family had a farm on Water Lane, mentions,

York and Ainsty Hunt 1911 at Clifton Green (Margaret Arnold)

My mother was really keen on horses and my dad was as well so they did a lot of riding with the York and Ainsty North Hunt. My mother was very friendly with Lady Chesterfield, used to ride out with her quite often.

It was before my time, it was '31, '32 when they went out riding. The farm had about six horse boxes but we kept mainly riding horses not carthorses. By the time the war came it was starting to die out a little bit. We had a lot of other things to worry about.

From the early 20th century, horses grazed on the Green from May to October and were still there in the 1980s. Once or twice horses escaped which was obviously dangerous. On the night of the Blitz in April 1942,

Joan Aherne recalls that,

> *Two or three horses were kept on the Green and I do remember these horses running around, absolutely terrified. I think somebody came and got them.*

Lena Mills recalls horses there in later years.

> *There have been horses on there occasionally, the gypsies put them on. They were wild and if you weren't careful, they'd attack you.*

Another highlight on the Green was the annual bonfire. Unfortunately Joan Aherne had an unpleasant experience.

> *One year somebody put a firework through the letterbox* [of their house 9 Clifton Green] *and burnt a coat behind it. After that we always boarded it up on Bonfire Night. I used to go upstairs and watch.*

And Lena Mills was

> *always frightened because the silly fools had crackers but the bonfire was terribly high. Those houses* [facing the Green] *must have been really frightened because sparks go flying. But it was well known through York. It was a big one.*

It became so famous that it was featured in November 1956 as part of a programme 'Remember Remember' on Granada TV. The interviewer was Des O'Connor who said that the aim of the programme was 'to bring to viewers all the fun of Guy Fawkes night just a few hundred yards from the school where Guy Fawkes was himself educated'. The bonfire was lit by Hilary Pinder from Knapton who rode round it twice on a white horse before igniting it by throwing on a blazing faggot. Major F C Beckwith, secretary of the Village Green Committee, explained that 'although the celebrations have been held for years and years and years, there has never been one like this before'. A torch parade of children, a choir and the Railway Institute band joined in the festivities. The programme also featured interviews with Clifton's oldest inhabitants, Thomas Plummer and Joan Aherne's grandfather, George Horner, both in their 80s.

Roy Hodgson remembers the bonfire.

It was quite an occasion. I think it got too dangerous for pedestrians and cars trying to get through so they decided they wouldn't do it anymore.

Joan Aherne recalls occasions when the Green was flooded. Her family had a piano when they lived at Clifton Green.

I remember getting four or five bricks in each corner. It was an old piano, quite a heavy one. As you went in the door it was on that wall so it would have got wet first. Luckily it was just lapping on the top step. It didn't flood inside, but it did in the one at the end of those three cottages.

There were bad floods in 1892, 1947, 1978 and again in more recent years. In the floods of 1947 Joan was actually featured in the press, when meeting her friend at the Green.

She lived down Burton Stone Lane and we were meeting round where the floods were and this photographer said, "You sit on there and we'll send the boat for you". There were lots of spectators.

On the road it was all right. We had wellies on. The road that runs at the bottom of the Green was deeper. The beck in Water Lane flooded, the river came up and that beck couldn't take it. It was flooded for quite a few days.

In 1963 there was a plan to divide the Green into three parts and eventually construct extra roads over it to form a traffic roundabout. This was to alleviate traffic resulting from the opening of the new Clifton Bridge. There was widespread opposition to this, including letters

Floods on Clifton Green 1947. Joan Aherne sitting on rail, on left with beret (Joan Aherne)

submitted by the York Civic Trust, and the scheme was shelved. A new system of traffic lights at the Water Lane-Clifton and the Water End-Clifton junctions was installed.

But in 1971 the Friends of Clifton Green (formed in 1969 as a fund raising group) recommended that the use of the Green by Shaw's Fair should cease. The Feast had become less popular, particularly with older people, because of the traffic, the noise and the mess left behind. In February 1972, Clifton residents decided by a narrow majority of 553 to 517 that they did not want the fair to continue. The City Council had reservations because of the rent paid to them by the fair proprietor, who offered to double it in order to keep the site, and in fact the Estates Committee wanted the fair to continue, but the full Council reversed their decision and agreed to go with the public referendum. So the annual fair came to an end.

In January 1975, the Clifton Green Residents' Association got £250 to drain and improve the Green, and a new drainage system was installed in September. In October, 1000 daffodil bulbs were planted. The Parks

Department regularly inspected the Green and in the summer of 1983, they decided that the trees needed thinning and tidying and the Radio Rentals aerial (erected in 1924) should be removed. Nearly 80 years after the meeting of prominent citizens about the future of the Green, a meeting was held that year by the Friends of Clifton Green to discuss the rotten elm tree. The city solicitor finally agreed that 'legal and financial responsibility lay with the City Council'. But the Friends did make a donation towards the cost of felling the tree. New trees were also planted (a small leaved lime and two beeches) and a Norway spruce came from the Forestry Commission's Wheldrake plantation. The Friends group continued to help fund the work and over the year 1983-4 their donations totalled £426. The committee consisted of Miss E Smallwood, Dr Kenneth Hutton, Mr B Braithwaite, Cyril Branchette, Director of Shepherd's Builders, Mr T Day and Professor Ian Pyle (professor of computer science at York University). Kenneth Hutton, who died in 1987, had set up a Kenneth Hutton Memorial Trust, with the income to go to the Clifton Green Committee.

Clifton Green in the snow (Derek Metcalfe)

Derek Metcalfe lives close to the Green.

The Green is for the use of the community of Clifton. I don't like all the trees that have been put on there, but some of them are memorial trees. The problem with this Green is, the roads are very busy all round it. We used to have Christmas trees on there, then they smashed all the bulbs.

We can negotiate way-leave across the Green, people who run cables underneath it, internet and telephone cables. They pay six pound odd a year for way-leave. And there's the big sewer goes under there, you can walk down it. The old Bur Dike ran across here and I remember them digging across the Green to lay the enormous pipes. It ran at the side of what was called Coffin Lane, because Clifton didn't have a church [until 1867] and they used to take all the coffins, unless you were wealthy, down the lane to St Olave's Church. Then you had the service there and off they went to the cemetery.

Clifton electro-bus at Clifton Green bus charging station (Hugh Murray)

At the front of Clifton Green is a small building which was a charging station for the battery powered buses which operated between Clifton and Stockton Lane from 1915 to 1923. It also included a waiting room. (There is a similar building at Stockton Lane roundabout, which is now used as a florist's shop).

Derek recalls,

> *It was then turned into a police box with a blue light when they wanted the policeman. Then they turned it into a bus shelter. It was getting abused and a certain councillor decided it should be a public toilet. Then the cuts came about and it was put on the market for a shop.*

In early 2011 it opened as a barber's shop, named The Gents, owned by Amy Willetts, with hairdresser Kara working there.

Kara the barber (Mike Race)

Barber's shop (Mike Race)

Today, the Green continues to be loved by all who live near it. No events take place there now, and it is a place of peace amidst all the nearby hustle and bustle. There are 37 trees there. Locals still get involved in caring for the Green and holding litter picking sessions, like members of Clifton Parish Church, including Pam Young,

> *We used to wash the railings before somebody would paint them. It's a hard task because you never got them as clean as you wanted. We'd be doing this with our buckets and you'd get people stop in the traffic jams and would go, "Good on you, mate, thank you for doing that". And of course you'd start laughing and talking. It was fun.*

– Chapter 3 –

HOUSES IN CLIFTON

There is a wide variety of housing in the Clifton area, ranging from the oldest almshouses, Ingram's Hospital, built in 1632, to the new council estates in Water Lane built three centuries later in the 1930s. There is also probably more variety of architectural style than any other area of York.

Clifton and Bootham are distinguished by a number of distinctive, attractive large houses, of 17th, 18th, 19th and 20th century origin. Many of these are now listed buildings. The Rowntree family properties and the big houses of Burton Stone Lane are covered in other chapters.

In 1836, land in Clifton was sold off by William Robinson and housing development began soon after. In 1861 there were 63 houses listed in the street directory for Clifton, though only three had numbers. Within a decade this had increased enormously. By 1900 most houses were numbered, though numbering has changed at least twice in the last century. Over the last 50 years, many blocks of houses have been acquired by St Peter's School, and a number of substantial houses in the roads off Clifton, like Queen Anne's Road, St Peter's Grove and Westminster Road, are now hotels and guesthouses.

BOOTHAM GRANGE

The Grange Hotel is number 1 Clifton. It is described as a classic regency townhouse, and was built in 1829 by two members of a wealthy ecclesiastical family, Rev William Richardson, who was a minister at St Michael le Belfrey, and his brother James, also a vicar.

Prior to the house being built, the land was a brickfield between the

Grange Hotel, No1 Clifton (*Christine Kyriacou*)

road and the river, run by Montague Giles in the 17th century. There are mentions of Roman discoveries there in the Ralph Thoresby collection of letters and a description of an ox roasting in 1698. The house was divided into two residences by the Richardsons, and James started off in the smaller house and moved into the bigger one after his brother's death. In 1851 James, his wife Elizabeth, five children, a parlour maid, cook, housemaid and under-maid were living there. In 1881 the two houses were occupied by Joseph Oldfield and William Henry Cobb. The Cobbs were a well connected York family. William Henry lived there with eight children and four servants, with the other half occupied by the Thompsons with eleven children!

William Cudworth, an engineer on the railway, lived at the house in 1900 when it was called Thornleigh. In 1920, John Hetherton changed the name to Bootham Grange, and converted the house into flats for family members. During the Second World War, service women lived in the flats, and there were air raid shelters in the cellar.

In 1989 Cassel Hotels bought the building and the celebrated Swiss interior designer, Christophe Gollut, was commissioned to create the Grange Hotel, with 36 bedrooms, which was awarded 'best newcomer of the North' by the AA hotel guide in 1991. The hotel extension of restaurant and conference facilities was completed in 1994. The owner Jeremy Cassel's grandfather, Sir Felix Cassel, was attorney general during the Second World War, and his father Sir Harold Cassel was an eminent QC and judge until he retired in 1990. His cousins include Lady Gowerie and Lady Pamela Hicks, daughter of Earl Mountbatten, Prince Rupert Loewenstein and Dr Muck Flick of Mercedes Benz.

Mary Cudworth, MBE, the daughter of William Cudworth, lived at the Grange in her younger days. She died aged 96 in 1979. She had been a Women's Citizen candidate for the Monk Ward in 1919 but was defeated. She had later taken various candidacies, became a JP in 1934 and retired

No 2 Clifton, home of Dr Cameron 1930s

from the bench in 1958. When she moved to 138 Clifton, next door but one to Clifton Church, Mary Morris helped to look after her.

> *She was a suffragette and a fascinating woman, she was really lovely. I quickly learnt that she was a very learned person and wanted the paper reading to her and then to discuss it. And she was used to having [meals] properly set with a damask tablecloth. Miss Cudworth's father had a temporary swimming pool [at Bootham Grange]. He was some high up so-and-so on the railway. I used to take her there in her wheelchair. She was blind but she said, "Oh yes, that used to be my sitting room".*

2 AND 4 CLIFTON

Two large three-bay town houses of three storeys and attics, which became 2 and 4 Clifton, were built soon after 1825 on land known as Bootham Garth or Coates' Closes, and purchased by Acaster Malbis Charity Trust.

Elizabeth Ogle c1860 (York Explore)

Harriet Ogle c1860 (York Explore)

The Ogle family, well-known in Clifton, lived at number 2 from the 1850s. Of the five siblings, Thomasin, Hannah Jane, Elizabeth, Harriet and their brother William, the last to survive were maiden ladies Elizabeth Ogle who died in 1870 and Harriet Ogle who died in 1876.

THE WHITE HOUSE AT NO 10 CLIFTON

This was built in about 1730, and bought by William Roberts, mercer. It then also included number 8. From 1828 to 1853, it was the home of the Rev Danson Richardson Currer, cleric and magistrate. He is listed as being 'without cure of souls' (ie. without a parish). The house was later heightened to three storeys, with five bays at the front. By the 1890s it had become the Post, Money Order, Telegraph and Savings Bank Office. In the 1930s it was the York telephone manager's office, who moved with his staff to buildings at Blackfriars House, Rougier Street, in January 1964. In 1965 it became the offices of the Royal Commission on Historical Monuments until 1989.

The White House 2011 (*Christine Kyriacou*)

CLIFTON VIEW

The two houses at 42 and 44 Clifton were built as one in the second half of the 18th century and divided into two about 1850. Number 42 was named Clifton View.

William Dowell, who wrote his memories of Clifton at the turn of the 20th century, recalls,

> *This was the home of Miss Maria Husband. The bedrooms on the top storey were turned into aviaries with large wire netting structures built out from the front windows. A very kind lady but she didn't consider boys knew how to care for pets. We had all kinds, kept at the stables in St Mary's, racing (homing) pigeons which we raced home from as far as Eastbourne, rabbits, guinea pigs, and best of all a Shetland pony, Dolly, the pride of my elder brother, and my donkey, Rosy, a large black Spanish ass. Miss Husband heard that we had acquired a beautiful owl and hurried to see father, telling me we weren't capable of looking after it. To our dismay we had to hand it over to her with the promise of a song bird in exchange but we didn't get one.*

> *Rosy was sold to Lord Deramore of Heslington Hall. He saw me riding one day and later told Father that Rosy was just the mount for his daughter. Despite my protests and tears, the old moke was sold and I had to be content with my first bicycle as a consolation.*

CLIFTON GARTH

William Dowell also remembers,

> *Colonel* [Felix Gottlieb Ludwig] *Schroeder resided in a large house* [called Clifton Garth] *between Clifton View and the Old Manor House. He was a retired cavalry officer and a buyer of horses for the German army. In association with Fred Ellis, my father bought and sold horses. On one occasion I accompanied him to Holland where*

I stayed for a month, after which we returned with 18 horses, great excitement for me watching them on and off trains and the ship. This was in April 1904.

Schroeder owned one of the six telephones in Clifton in 1891, number 76. A few years after his wife's death in 1903, he moved to live at 3 Burton Villas in Burton Stone Lane, where he filed for bankruptcy in 1909.

MARY ELLEN BEST

Mary Ellen Best, the well-known watercolour artist, was a resident of Clifton. There has been some confusion as to which house she lived in, as she was listed at number 1 Clifton, and later number 14, but neither of these seemed to fit with her paintings of the interior and the garden of her house. In 1983 her painting of the family in her Clifton garden in 1883 was sold at auction with 46 other pictures. In 1998, the Yorkshire Evening Press reported that number 44, which was on the market for £285,000, had been the artist's house, and the garden at the rear, with its lawn and flower beds, and fruit and vegetable area, could be identified by the gate pillars. The house was built in the late 18th century, incorporating some earlier parts from 1696, and is now a Grade II listed property. Mary Ellen was the daughter of Dr Charles Best, a physician at Bootham Park Hospital. In 1840 she married John Sarg of Nuremberg and they moved to Germany.

CLIFTON GREEN HOUSE AND COWL'S YARD

In 1883 the deeds of Clifton Green House described 'a parcel of land south west of the village green on which are ten dwelling houses, extending to the public footpath to Marygate Hamlet, then used as a market garden occupied by Henry Cowl, who also occupies one of the dwellings'. The 1850 Ordnance Survey map shows Clifton Green House with Cowl's Yard next to it. The Yard was named after Thomas Cowl. William Cowl, who had been living at 29 Clifton as a gardener when he was sixteen, became a florist and seedsman, and he, and his two brothers Henry and George, had a share in the yard, all being descended

Cowl family 1916-17. Back row – Harry, Edie, Jennie, Lizzi, Jim
Middle Row – Kitty, Mother (Hannah), Florrie and Father (Robert)
Front – Glen, Keith's father (with present for brother Bob in hospital in France) and Alice
(Keith Cowl)

from Thomas. The land at the back, which was used as a market garden, stretched back to Love Lane, (which ran behind St Peter's School right to Marygate). Henry's great grandson, Keith Cowl, explains,

There were ten freehold cottages known as Cowl's Cottages, and a market garden behind, occupied by Henry Cowl and others. Henry was born in Clifton but lived in Sunderland at one time, where there was probably family. He married Mary Anne Glen and brought her back to Clifton with her two young daughters, Isabella and Mary, from her first marriage. Isabella gave birth to a son in Cowl's Yard.

Love Lane with Queen Anne's School

The cottages housed farm labourers, a weaver, shopkeeper, butler and two widows, one working in the garden. William Cowl died in 1872 at the young age of 37, and left his share of the property in trust for his widow Annie, until it passed to his five year old son Charles when he reached 21. After his brother George died in 1878, leaving his share to his wife, there was a dispute over the ownership.

There were three brothers involved, there was a bit of squabbling. You know when wills...property...I think they fell out about it. In those days a lady...they didn't have rights. There was somebody looking after her [George's widow] *business-wise, guarding her rights.*

Annie and Henry Cowl disputed the claim of George's widow. Finally the family entered into an agreement in 1880, dividing the property into 15 shares between Henry Cowl, and Rev James Wayman and Isaac Wilde who held the shares in trust for William's widow Annie, and George's widow, Esther.

It was sold for £1000, conveyanced by Hepper and Kaye, and my great grandfather, Henry, got £330 as a share.

Henry was living at number 10 Cowl's Yard with nine cottages occupied by labourers and grooms. After selling his share, he continued to live there until shortly before his death in 1903 of 'dropsy'. Henry's eldest son Robert, Keith's grandfather, went to work on the railway but his younger son Arthur continued in the business and was a proprietor of the nursery and market garden in 1908. Keith explains

Gardening seems to have been in the family. Philip Cowl, who I knew at Acomb Secondary Modern School when I was a pupil, he was the gardening teacher as well as an interest in sport, which is similar to myself and the rest of the family. My father had an allotment at Bustardthorpe and I've taken it over from him.

The land and ten cottages were advertised for sale by auction in June 1881. There were several owners before the builder Henry Colman bought it in 1901 and converted Clifton Green House into two dwelling houses. This included what is now the Hotel Noir on Clifton Green. One house had classrooms which had been used as a residence and boarding house for St Peter's School, the other had been used for Dr Belcombe's Asylum (see chapter on Doctors and Hospitals). Colman also developed what had been Lord Robert's Road and this all became Clifton Dale.

HOUSES IN WATER END

In the early 19th century, much of Water End, the road leading from the main street in Clifton, to the river at Clifton Scope, was farmland. Most of it belonged to the Holgate family. The 1849 map shows Clifton Croft, Clifton Holme, the Sycamore Inn (later Sycamore Cottage), the Marquee, the lodge or gardener's cottage of Clifton Croft, (later called Roper's Lodge), Ousecliffe, Cliff Hill (later Haverford) and the Homestead. The last two are covered in the chapter on the Homestead.

Clifton Croft

CLIFTON CROFT

A grade II listed building, Clifton Croft was built in 1830 for John Roper, a wine merchant, who was then aged 25, on land bought from the Holgates. The house is in white brick with a curved Tuscan entrance porch, with Regency cornices in the rooms and St Francis in the stained glass lighting the staircase. Roper died in 1875. He had gone into partnership with James Melrose in 1861 and left the house to him. Melrose was a well known character in York, who was always seen dressed in black with a silk top hat. On Sundays he went to the Minster in a brougham. He was director of Yorkshire Insurance, York Gas Company, Barclays Bank, York Cemetery Company, and chairman of York County Savings Bank and York Race Committee. He was also treasurer for York County Hospital, and was a freemason for over 75 years. He was a magistrate and was Lord Mayor in 1876. After his wife Elizabeth's death in 1899, Melrose had a stained glass window built in memoriam to her in Clifton Parish Church, with the words, 'This woman was full of good works and alms deeds which she did'. When he reached the age of 100 in 1928, a service of thanksgiving was held at St Lawrence's Church for him. He died the following year and his funeral was held in the Minster. His sons Walter, John and William sold the house and grounds to Robert James Pulleyn for building land. Pulleyn was still living in the house in December 1937, and sold it to two doctors, Edward and Henrietta Ball-Dodd. But he had begun to develop the land in the late 1920s and early '30s, and Greencliffe Drive, Ousecliffe Gardens and Westminster Road were created.

ROPER'S LODGE, 16 Clifton Green

Roper's Lodge was built as the gardener's cottage, an interesting example of secular Gothic revival as applied to a small dwelling.

Roper's Lodge (Derek Metcalfe)

Derek Metcalfe explains.

It was built for the owner of the estate, John Roper. John gave his gardener a nice house and looked after him well. The windows were put in later, they weren't an original feature. The coins around the window certainly add to the Gothic style, the Pugin style. Pugin designed a lot of Gothic revival properties in Victorian times. Attached to it is a four cornered spiral staircase with pointed view and weather vane on it. Architecturally it's a marvellous piece of workmanship, with two slate windows which you would probably find in a nice castle. If anyone was attacking you could put out your bow and arrow.

In Georgian times, you got the wealthy people moving out of the city, the slums as such, wealthy people like the Munbys, the Ropers and one or two other people, bought their little villas. Earl De Grey, when the railways started coming to York, wanted to sell his land to plough his money, to the best of my knowledge, into the railways. The people in York were allowed to buy the parcels of land of Clifton. Initially the pasture people were people like the Marquee Inn, the Sycamore, the White House, the Grey Mare, the Burton Stone. They were all inns that had horses. And when they bought the houses, they had the legal right to graze their cattle on this ground.

The house goes back to 1846, the boundary stone. The driveway to his house was where Greencliffe Drive is. All the land that he owned was sold to Pulleyn the builder. John Mitchell, the archivist of Bootham School, took over the Lodge and sympathetically

Derek Metcalfe (Derek Metcalfe)

restored it, with my advice in the background. He loved it and we kept all his original features.

Many passers-by mistake it for an old church.

[Before the parish church was built], *there was no church, and it was used for religious meetings. The Roper's arms are on the side of the house in stone.*

CLIFTON HOLME

Clifton Holme (Mike Race)

Clifton Holme is situated in Ousecliffe Gardens, a large two storey rectangular block with a porch of three bays and a lower servants' wing. It was first owned by Joseph Munby, for whom it was built in 1848. He was a solicitor and amateur musician, who was the organist at St Martin's for over 15 years and on the management committee of the York Choral and Philharmonic Society. He was appointed Master Extraordinary of the

High Court of Chancery in 1832. Munby died in 1875 aged 71 and is laid to rest in the family vault with his wife of 48 years, Caroline Eleanor who died at Clifton Holme in 1879, and two of his sons, John Forth Munby, captain in the 1st West Yorkshire Volunteers who died in 1872 aged 41, and his brother Joseph Edwin, a 'clerk in holy orders' who died in 1867 aged 27. There is a memorial plaque to them in Clifton Parish Church.

The eldest son, Arthur Joseph Munby, was born in 1828. He was educated at St Peter's School and Trinity College, Cambridge. Afterwards, he read for the Bar, more at his father's insistence than from any desire to practise law. He became a poet and started to have his work published in 1878.

Over the next decades, Munby, working as a minor civil servant in London, kept detailed journals about his meetings with artistic and literary celebrities, (he was an acquaintance of Darwin, Swinburne, Thackeray and Dickens), but he also had a deep interest in poor working women. He kept diaries describing girls he met on the street or in their workplaces. He began to travel the country sketching, photographing, and interviewing plough-girls and pit-girls, milkmaids and fisherwomen, female sailors and acrobats, as well as prostitutes. In 1854 he met, and later secretly married, Hannah Cullwick, a maid of all work. He kept up the pretence that Hannah was his housekeeper and she always called him Massa (Master). He liked her to blacken her face with black lead to look like a chimney sweep.

Munby died in 1910 but his diary and much of his correspondence were not opened until 1950, revealing 'a bizarre and fascinating double life'. The diaries recorded his meetings and interviews with young women over the course of 40 years as his obsession continued. One night in 1888, he was accosted by a group of men who accused him of being Jack the Ripper. At that time, many solitary gentlemen were being accused of the Whitechapel murders. He was thought to fit the description as he wandered alone at night, was well dressed and respectable and he talked to young women on the streets. But there is no evidence that his interest went further than that. Several books have been written about the relationship of Munby and Hannah Cullwick, and a TV drama documentary shown in 2008. The main reason was because the couple had broken the strict Victorian codes. A relationship, and much less a marriage, between a man of his class and a maid, would have probably resulted in him losing his job and his place in society.

Clifton Holme was advertised for sale in September 1907. In 1919 it was bought by York Penitentiary Society, which had been established since 1822, to become a home for young women in need aged 14-17 to 'shelter girls who have temporarily got into difficulties...and be instrumental in persuading girls and women to lead respectable lives'. Their premises in Bishophill had become dilapidated and they needed a new property. They had to build a modern laundry for the women to work in, more bathrooms and sleeping accommodation for 30. The home was run by a matron, kitchen matron and a laundress, and governed by a management committee which included local men of means like Oscar Rowntree, David Russell of Clifton Lodge, William Whytehead and Sir James Meek, as well as an honorary chaplain, doctor and dentist. There was also a ladies' committee who helped to fundraise, mostly the wives of local landowners such as Mrs Bowes Morrell and Elizabeth Melrose. The home was compared to a 'lifeboat for drowning women and girls.'

The girls were encouraged to take part in activities organised by the Guide movement. These included singing, folk dancing, needlework, drill, handicrafts, nature study, hygiene, physiology and ambulance work. There were occasional trips to garden parties, the annual Gala in Bootham, on the river and to matinees at the cinemas.

The income to run the home came partly from donations and subscriptions, but mainly from the laundry work. In 1923 the committee decided to alter the premises from a power laundry back to a hand laundry, abolish the boiler and return to having fires under the coppers, because of the costs incurred. But by 1936 the home was in financial trouble, with a large overdraft. The annual cost of running the property was £2300 (including salaries which were £289, laundry costs £354 and housekeeping £694).

St Hilda's Garth children's home 1950s (York Oral History Society)

In August 1939 it was converted to a 'Home Office School for Girls of 15 on admission', but, after the Second World War, Clifton Holme became St Hilda's Garth, a children's home, until the 1970s. The council-run Glen Residential Nursery was built further down Ousecliffe Gardens.

Today Clifton Holme is once again the private home of a lawyer, and part of the grounds has become Clifton Holme Court and Clifton Holme Mews.

GREEN TREE COTTAGE, 28 WATER END/THE WHITE HOUSE

Built in the early 19th century, this house was called the Green Tree in 1830 and owned in 1851 by George Holgate, a farmer with 57 acres. In 1836 it became the Sycamore Inn kept by Alice Holgate. This house is now called the White House, Water End.

Sycamore Inn, Water End 1929 (Hugh Murray)

GREY GABLES, 7 WATER END

Caroline Abbott Derby, an American lady, born in Boston, Massachusetts in 1873, bought Grey Gables at 7 Water End, on the corner of Westminster Road, in the 1920s. Archabel Little, a local person, became her companion. When Caroline died in August 1945 aged 72, she left the house to Archabel. As the latter grew older, her niece and husband came to live with and look after her, and following her death in February 1965 at the age of 89, they inherited the house. Several owners later, the house was demolished to make way for a rather unusual building, which looks a little like a church, with one side of glass. There were local objections but, in the end, planning permission was given. As it is on the corner of Water End and Westminster Road, it now has the number Zero Westminster Road!!

During the building of the new house, the contractors found a letter behind the fireplace, addressed to, 'Whoever finds this in the wall'. It reads

This house was completed in February 1933, for me (Miss) Caroline Abbott Derby, aged 59 years, 10m. My friend (Miss) Archabel Little also lives here with me. We hope whoever finds this note in after years will have a happy home here, and remember the first occupants. Do not be afraid of us, if we 'come back' with our little dog Timmy, we are kindly 'ghosts'. God bless you all, Caroline A Derby.

Marion Tweedy was born in Ousecliffe Gardens in 1931. She explains,

They lived like ladies. Miss Derby was always in dove grey or lavender. Very Edwardian. Miss Derby must have been 'nicely thank you', Miss Little was just ordinary. One had more money and provided the home and the other probably organised things. It's an interesting social thing. There were an awful lot of single women following the First World War, this is the sort of thing that happened.

Caroline Derby and Archabel Little 1930 (Marion Tweedy)

OUSECLIFFE AND GOVERNMENT HOUSE ROAD

Ousecliffe was built in the 19th century. William Hudson, the registrar, occupied it for a number of years until he moved to Burton Cottage shortly before his death in 1864. In 1900 the house was occupied by Richard Lawson who also had three cottages for his butler, groom and stud groom. The house eventually became Government House and the lane leading up to it, Government House Road. The lane leading to Clifton Holme is actually Ousecliffe Gardens. At the bottom of Ousecliffe Gardens is the St Peter's School football and rugby ground.

Marion Tweedy recalls,

There were not Westminster Road houses then. It was fields and cows in them. Clifton was beginning to be a suburb. There were one or two little farmsteads. Then they were pulled down. The footpath coming up Water End was next to the road. Government House was the big house and then there were three, one a bit bigger and two smaller, all belonging to the army. In one of them lived Celia and Audrey Wigg. And their father became Lord Wigg eventually. He was something to do with racing.

A lot of mystery seems to surround Government House Road which, even today, is a private road. There has always been a connection with the civil service and probably the army. One lady who worked there as a cleaner in the 1960s had to sign the Official Secrets Act to stop her discussing any paperwork she might find there.

Marion Tweedy 2011 (Van Wilson)

At Government House they had garden parties. My mother said that one year Princess Royal of Harewood House was there. We could look over our fence and down at them and see what was happening. And then came the war, they built Nissen huts for the army in the back, and Italian prisoners were working on them.

Sheila Goater also recalls,

If you went to the theatre at night you often used to see the Government House people. You could tell who they were because they were all dressed better than anyone, probably in evening dress.

Of the nine homes now on Government House Road, six are much newer houses. According to local estate agents, it is one of the more expensive parts of York.

Numbers 39, 41 and 43 Water End were built in 1849, supposedly to house domestic staff of Government House. They are now demolished.

ELLISON'S TERRACE

On the other side of Water End, facing the Green, is Ellison's Terrace, which was built for John Ellison, 'landed proprietor' in the mid-19th century, on land owned originally by the Holgates but which had been sold to the Ellisons, a farming family dating back to the 17th century. John lived in a farm on the site but built the terrace around it. When the land came up for sale in the early 20th century, there were seven lots, including piggeries, greenhouses, a paddock and six houses. There was a back road behind them, which came out on Shipton Road. Next to the Terrace was the site of the proposed new almshouses which was bought by John Burrill.

DUTCH HOUSE, SHIPTON ROAD

The Dutch House (Van Wilson)

Jacob Simon Gans moved to York from his native Holland, and transferred his button factory, Gansolite, to Haxby Road in 1930. Peter Rowntree became one of the directors. Gans lived briefly at Clifton Lodge and later moved next door to the Dutch House on Shipton Road. He died in 1952. The company was taken over by United Button Corporation in 1961. In 1990 it employed 70 people and was making an average of five million buttons a week, which made it the biggest button maker in Britain.

THE NEW ESTATES AND THEIR BUILDERS

Reg Pulleyn was the contractor responsible for building much of the Clifton Croft estate. He was a labour councillor, Lord Mayor in 1939 and received the BEM (British Empire Medal) in the 1960s. His brother Vic Pulleyn owned Clifton Garage, which had previously been the Lofthouse's garage (see chapter on Shops and Businesses).

Henry Colman was also a prominent builder in Clifton, and owned a saw mill and yard in Avenue Road. He built houses on the town side of Avenue Terrace, having bought 70 Clifton, a three storey house with a garden the length of Avenue Road. The house was reduced by one storey and a row of houses appeared on the land which had been his garden. 89 Clifton Green, now numbers 8 and 11, was also once owned by the Colmans. The firm had an office and showroom in Bootham, next to Priestley's butchers. This became the second shop of Dandy's bakers.

Extensive building took place in the 1930s. People who were rehoused when some of the Hungate, Layerthorpe and Walmgate streets were demolished went largely to Tang Hall and Clifton. The new houses were modern with electricity, indoor toilets and gardens. Birch's and Shepherd's were some of the builders involved. As many of the people were Catholics, (descendants of the Irish community in Walmgate), St Joseph's Church was built for them in Crichton Avenue.

Doug Heald lived for a few years in Kingsway from 1943 to 1951, when it was a fairly new estate.

I was born in the Kingsway North area. Now it's Burton Green. That would be 1943. I can remember happy times because we had the fields at the back, and the green which is in the middle, we used to play on there. It was as even as it is now, and tree-lined. It was used like a dump, where the soil heaps were put before the Second World War. They were obviously going to continue a road, the outer bypass I believe. The war brought it to an end. Towards the Wigginton Road side, there was a hill which we used to call the tip, all earth from the excavations from the Kingsway North streets. Everyone used to go sledging in the winter and enjoying the summer fields on top of the hill.

Water Lane street sign *(Christine Kyriacou)*

Streets in the Kingsway area were named after local personages. Crombie Avenue was named after the Crombie family, freemen of York since 1810. Solicitor Norman Crombie lived at Haverford on Water End until his death in 1937. Annie and George Crombie, who was a commissioner for oaths, lived at Ouselea at the beginning of the 20th century.

Malcolm Maher was born in 1937 in Spalding Avenue.

Kingsway wasn't there then. Peterhill was there, Philip's Grove was there, and Water Lane. And Burdike was there. They were built after Spalding Avenue.

We played out all the time in that area. There were no cars at all. The only person we used to see was Plummer's farm. We moved to Kingsway. On that corner there was 218 [Burton Stone Lane], *the very last house, that's where we went. We was there maybe four years. My mother never locked the door. We used to say, "Weren't you frightened of anybody coming in and pinching owt?" She said, "We didn't have anything to pinch". It's like a community. I loved it down there. I don't know people's names down this street and we've been here 50 years, but I could take you down Spalding Avenue and I can tell you everybody's name that lived in them houses.*

If you walked down the street and there was an older couple, you moved off. If you said anything or got nasty to somebody, your parents wouldn't allow you. It was a different set-up altogether. I knew everybody down Peterhill, St Philip's Grove. They all went to our school. I think nearly everybody was poor when I lived down there. Once you got to the end of Burdike and that bend, that was Rawcliffe Lane. They were rich, to us. Opposite the Mitre, that big white house was the police house. He was a good copper actually. He'd come on t'bike and if you did anything wrong, he'd catch you and give you a slap.

You had pushbikes but one you got off your mates or borrowed. Jimmy Barker and me used to have a trolley, we went for cinders for t'fire, where Foss Islands is, there used to be a place there. We went there and got the cinders with a sack.

A lot of the rituals and sense of community that had existed in the inner city places like Hungate were taken to the new estates. The men continued to play pitch and toss in the streets, only running away when the local policeman came. They listened more to the local priest who would visit everyone and knew all their families.

Gerald Barker remembers,

Kingsway being built. I used to walk up there to Haxby Road School. I remember a gate falling on my foot because things weren't finished. I was having a nosey. They were iron gates. I remember getting a scraped shin. But if you took all the housing that was built from about 1934, '35, away from anywhere in York, York becomes relatively small. It's interesting the way that York has progressed. When the railway came, the population doubled or trebled in no time. Unfortunately it's now got too big. It's become an uncomfortable place, it's not built for modern times.

– Chapter 4 –

THE HOMESTEAD
AND ROWNTREE PROPERTIES

In the early years of the 20th century, members of the Rowntree family, well known as chocolate manufacturers and Quakers in York, owned several large properties on the edge of Clifton.

Bill Sessions was born in York in 1915, studied economics at Cambridge and returned to run the family business of Sessions printers and publishers until his retirement. He had connections with the Rowntree family before they moved into chocolate.

> *The Rowntrees spread from Pavement in the middle of York out*
> *towards first Bootham and then Clifton. They were busy and active*
> *grocers. Joseph Rowntree gave his income for the three big Rowntree's*
> *trusts. They were Quakers and they took Quaker household*
> *apprentices. One of those was my grandfather, William Sessions.*

HAVERFORD

The house now called Haverford on Water End in Clifton, next to Clifton Scalp, (later Clifton Scope), was bought in 1842 as a home for William Catton, a woollen draper of High Ousegate, who lived there with his wife Mary and several servants. In 1851 he employed one man and one boy. It was named Cliff Hill, but became Cliff Villa when Catton sold it to Henry Hillyard. By April 1899 the house was occupied by Major the Honourable O V Lumley, and was sold again at an auction taking place at Harker's Hotel. The house contained three reception rooms, servants' hall, 'arched and commodious cellars', six bedrooms and dressing room, bathrooms

Haverford (Derek Metcalfe)

and two servants' bedrooms. A flagged courtyard adjoined the house with the butler's room, out offices and a small greenhouse. In the stable yard were three coach houses, saddle room and looseboxes, cow house, hay stores, boiler house, and gardener's room with bedroom above. A large vinery, greenhouses, potting houses and a shed completed the buildings. The slopes towards the river were 'well wooded and fenced', and the flower gardens contained a Gothic arch and rockery. By the beginning of the 20th century, it was bought by Francis (Frank) Henry Rowntree, managing director of Rowntree's and great-nephew of Joseph Rowntree. He named it Haverford after the town in Pennsylvania, USA, where there is a big Quaker community.

After Frank died in 1918 at the age of 49, his wife Emily lived in the house. There were other families there until it was sold to the Joseph Rowntree Village Trust in 1945. It is described as a wonderful family home, with a large garden, stables, tennis court, orchards, and a rookery. The RAF used part of the building during the Second World War, but Frank's daughter Frieda and her husband George Harris also lived there. Marion Tweedy, who lived in nearby Ousecliffe Gardens, recalls playing with the children of the Harris family there.

*They had a sort of railway on a switchback. Of course they had more
money and we liked to go over and play.*

A bomb fell in the grounds in 1941 incurring damage to the roof,
windows and doors. After the war, the Trust leased it to the Youth Hostel
Association. By this time, Joseph's grandson Peter Rowntree was living
next door at the Homestead. The hostel opened officially as the Peter

Rowntree Memorial
Hostel on the 8th May
1948, with members
of the Rowntree family,
and many dignitaries,
from home and
abroad, attending. Peter
Rowntree, who retired
from the family firm in
1964, continued family
links by being president
of the Yorkshire
Regional Group of
the Youth Hostel
Association until 1972.

Youth Hostel plaque (Mike Race)

The building was extended in the 1950s and there was a re-opening
ceremony in 1959 by Richard Schirrman, who founded the youth hostel
movement in Germany in 1909. Many other hostels in the country
have closed in the last 20 years for financial reasons but the York one is
successful. Originally youth hostels catered for the 18-35 age group but, in
2005, the Charities Commission insisted that they be more open in their
policy. The York hostel welcomes families and individuals of any age. It
has a restaurant, bar, shop, laundry, games room and 37 bedrooms. Lucy
Staples lives nearby.

*My niece who lived down at Bexhill-on-Sea, their school would come
up every year when she was quite small. It's very nice in there. A
few years ago I went across because one of my great nephews was
there. They sat me down and brought me a cup of coffee and were*

very friendly people. It's certainly very busy. There were two girls who came from Hong Kong who were down by the river taking photographs and I started talking to them. Then I said, "If you want to come for a cup of tea...", and they thought it was wonderful to come into an English house.

THE MANOR HOUSE

At number 66 Clifton, just past Petersway, is the distinctive Manor House, built in the late 17th century, incorporating parts of an earlier timber framed structure which is probably 16th century but was damaged during the Civil War. The house has Dutch gables and Oriel windows. It was partly rebuilt in 1962.

William Dowell recalls

Mr Cooke, the scientific instrument maker, owner of Cooke, Troughton and Simms, lived in a large house near the corner of Avenue Terrace and we were friendly with his son and frequently met in the old Manor House, mostly playing table tennis, known in those days as ping pong.

In 1861 the Manor was owned by George Hicks Seymour, Lord Mayor of York in 1849. He was the Mayor when a banquet was given in the Guildhall in honour of Prince Albert, when he came to York.

The Manor House was split into two houses by the 1920s. Derek Metcalfe explains,

There used to be three houses there. They pulled the end one down to build Petersway. The left hand side of Avenue Terrace was built with Victorian houses, the bottoms built with Edwardian houses and there used to be an orchard and a tennis court. The orchard was taken up and houses were built on it. A guy called [Henry] Colman built those houses. The Manor House is all oak beams, a mish-mash of all sorts, and different floors, because it's been two houses.

Clifton Manor House c1930 (Hugh Murray)

Clifton Manor House 2011 (Van Wilson)

Joseph Rowntree's brother, Henry Isaac Rowntree, had several grand-daughters, Frieda, Madge, Faith Stainton Rowntree and her sister Nora, known as Nonie, the sisters of Frank Rowntree who lived at Haverford. Faith lived in the larger Manor House, and Nonie lived with her husband Major Ison in the house next door, on the corner of Petersway (which had once been a master's house for St Peter's School). The Manor House and some effects were bequeathed by Nora Rowntree Ison to the York Civic Trust in 1984. Bill Sessions knew the sisters.

Faith and Nonie Rowntree (and a parrot), a corking couple. They donated the house to the York Civic Trust. And then the Trust asked permission in more recent times to sell it and turned it into investments. They had a wonderful sister, Frieda, who married George Harris, the Sales Director of Rowntree's cocoa works. He had a great deal to do with starting Kitkat in the 1930s.

Edna Crichton, York's first woman Lord Mayor in 1941, lived at 66 Clifton in the 1950s (next door to Faith and Nonie Rowntree). She was made an honorary freeman of York in 1955, only the second woman to receive the honour, after the Princess Royal in 1952. Her husband David Crichton who died in 1921, had been the welfare officer at Rowntree's for many years. Both were councillors, and Crichton Avenue at the end of Burton Stone Lane, was named after him.

CLIFTON LAWN

Clifton Lawn on Shipton Road was occupied at the beginning of the 20th century by Walter Waddington, (of W Waddington and Sons) and George Potter-Kirby. A few years later, the latter had left and Theodore Hotham Rowntree, the nephew of Joseph and brother of Arnold Rowntree, and his wife Lucy were living there. The couple celebrated their golden wedding at the house in February 1948. Theodore died the following year aged 82 and is buried in the Friends' Burial Ground in Heslington Road.

CLIFTON LODGE

Clifton Lodge, on the corner of Shipton Road and Rawcliffe Lane, with its stately entrance and long wooded driveway, was built in 1852 by a York solicitor David Russell who died there in 1881. In 1884 it was sold to the Hon Reginald Parker and his wife Katherine. They had two daughters, Doreen, and Ethel who became Lady Ethel Thomson, and wrote about her childhood in her book 'Clifton Lodge'. In 1891, the Hon Reginald owned one of the 90 telephones in the city. There were six in Clifton and his telephone number was 60!

Lady Ethel's memoirs include a wonderful description of a Clifton which is now long gone.

Clifton Lodge where Joseph Rowntree lived (Joseph Rowntree Foundation)

Clifton Lodge Gates (Van Wilson)

Once upon a time Clifton had been a village, flourishing round its Green. Its antiquity could be vouched for by evidence in the fields which my father had acquired with the cottage and farm buildings adjoining his property. He put his butler into the cottage and his jersey cow into the byre. One shed contained peat moss and sundry stores, another was loaned to me for my rabbits. The fields (11 acres) were wide ridge and furrow, proof of Early English small holdings that were tilled by the villagers in ancient times.

Our walks, taken twice a day, were usually up the 'Asylum Road' [Shipton Road] where hedges and green fields and a few villas with gardens led up to the big iron gates and railings which flanked the entrance to the North Riding Asylum. We used to see gangs of men working in the fields under the supervision of their guards, who wore navy blue suits and peaked caps. They threw turnips into farm carts. From the road we stood to watch the rhythm of the performance

55

and heard the 'Gee Wo' and 'Ah Wey' to the horse between the shafts. Sometimes a party of women would be met, chaperoned by keepers, taking the air. Some would laugh inanely and give us weird greetings, while others would walk along with bent heads. Small shawls formed the covering for their heads. It was a distressing sight.

One day when we were two miles up Asylum Road, and I was riding while the others walked with the governess, we saw approaching the large landau drawn by a spanking pair of high-stepping black horses belonging to Captain Robert Vyner, late Grenadier Guards, of Newby Hall. He owned the small estate of Fairfield near the village of Skelton. Here were his racing stables. We could often see yearlings running loose in the paddocks.

Music in the streets was provided by barrel organs. Each had its personnel of two to turn the handle, and they came up to Clifton on different days of the week. Having often been sent away from the front of the house, they would gain entry through the stable gates up the back lane, trundle the organ into our cobbled yard and begin grinding out their wheezy tunes in front of the kitchen window. The servants would be dancing and, in our bedroom above, we were doing the same. We would throw some of our scanty hoard of pence to the men, who greeted us with smiles and grins. We never heard them speak so they must have been foreigners, dark and swarthy looking fellows, and we imagined that in their own country, they were assuredly brigands and desperadoes.

On Sunday mornings we attended Clifton church for matins, and a hired four wheeled cab from Myton's stables in Bootham would take the parents to the Minster.

Various people came to stay for York or Doncaster races. Lord Feversham, who had come from Helmsley by train, took a four wheeled cab from York Station and drove up to Clifton Lodge with his tin hip bath carried on the roof. Another visitor confessed to never going anywhere away from home without a mouse-trap.

Joseph Rowntree bought Clifton Lodge in 1905 and lived there until his death in 1925. He built Rawcliffe Holt next door, on the Shipton Road side, for his youngest daughter Winifred and her husband Arthur Duncan Naish after their marriage in 1907. There was a connecting door between the two houses on the first floor. Sadly Winifred died in 1915 aged only 30. Joseph's second wife Emma Seebohm (sister of his first wife Julia Seebohm who had died aged only 22) died a year before him. Both houses were left to the Joseph Rowntree Trust. Quaker visitors and children from the Quaker schools, The Mount and Bootham, were often invited for meals and parties there, including Bill Sessions.

Rawcliffe Holt had a big garden, there was a tennis court, you could ride a cycle round perilous bends. There was a big thatched roofed [pavilion], which was used for community purposes. The mothers got together and the kiddies played outside and it was very happy.

In June 1916, Joseph Rowntree presented a 30-40 hp Studebaker five seater car for the use of the motor ambulance section of the York Voluntary Aid detachment for the period of the war. After his death at the age of 88, the gardens and land adjoining the two houses became the Clifton Lodge Estate, designed by Barry Parker of Letchworth, the Trust's architect from 1919 until his death in 1946. The 1926 plan showed 69 houses, as well as tennis courts, ponds, and gardens filled with trees, although fewer houses were actually built. The houses, which were built over the next ten years, varied in size. The first type had four bedrooms, dining room, sitting room, kitchen, scullery, fuel store, hall and loggia, with bathroom and downstairs cloakroom. There were also three-bedroomed and five-bedroomed houses. Bill Sessions lives in Rawcliffe Grove which

was at the bottom of his garden. At the back is a line of big trees, with a Turkey oak tree, quite unusual. Several of us joke that we are on the site of his pigsties. Under the trees, not very propitious for growing flowers, there's an absolute carpet, in the middle of February, of yellow aconites interspersed with snowdrops. It is very fertile ground. My school friend had had his home at Rawcliffe Holt at one time. He said, "It's an absolute tragedy, these new flats on the beautiful sunken rose garden of Rawcliffe Holt". He wouldn't drive past for years because he was so upset about it.

Another great nephew of Joseph Rowntree, Christopher, moved from his home in St Peter's Grove to one of the flats in Riseborough House in the 1960s, which was one of the new buildings in the grounds of Clifton Lodge. Previously he had lived at 6½ St Peter's Grove and was vice chairman of York City Magistrates. Next door to Riseborough House, at 5 Rawcliffe Lane, was the Catherine Cappe Memorial Trust Girls' Hostel, for young unmarried mothers. Catherine Cappe was a local benefactor who campaigned for worthy causes in the city and introduced a system of hospital visitors to reduce abuse and neglect. She was also involved with the Grey Coat School for Girls in York, and is said to be the only non-conformist interested in education in York in the 18th century. She was the wife of Rev Newcombe Cappe, pastor of the 'protestant dissenters' in the St Saviourgate chapel who died in 1800. She herself died in 1821 aged 77, but the Catherine Cappe Memorial Trust, for women and girls in hardship and distress, still exists. In 1963, the Yorkshire Evening Press reported that the girls' hostel at Rawcliffe Holt was in serious financial trouble.

Pam Young knew the house.

> *When we were at Queen Anne's, we knew that was a home for 'naughty girls', obviously girls who became pregnant. When I was in Greencliffe Drive, there was a couple called Lucy and Roy Davison, they had been the houseparents who ran that place. A lovely couple, social workers.*

Roy Hodgson recalls that the Hostel

> *caught fire in the '80s. They looked out of the window and the flames were 50 foot high. It burned down, nobody was killed. They rebuilt it, it's a children's nursery now. You got Shipton Road as the western boundary, Rawcliffe Lane as the eastern boundary, and Malton Way*

as the northern boundary, so it's really a triangle. It was all orchards [before the estate was developed].

Today the grounds of Clifton Lodge, on the Shipton Road side, stretch down for some metres, and from the outside the houses cannot be seen, only woodland.

Five Rowntrees c1920
L to R – Joseph Stephenson Rowntree, B Seebohm Rowntree, Joseph Rowntree, Arnold Stephenson Rowntree, Oscar Frederick Rowntree
(Joseph Rowntree Foundation)

THE HOMESTEAD

The fourth of Joseph Rowntree's seven children, Benjamin Seebohm Rowntree, bought three acres of land behind Cliff Villa (Haverford) from Henry Hillyard in 1904 and had a house built, by his cousin, Arts and Crafts architect Fred Rowntree of Scarborough, which he called the

Homestead. Fred was also responsible for work on the Rowntree's factory, the pavilion at Rawcliffe Holt, extensions at Bootham School and the Mount School, the layout of Rowntree Park in 1919, and many other properties throughout England and Scotland.

Seebohm Rowntree announced in the Yorkshire Gazette that from 18th July to 8th August 1904, the field behind his house would be available as a playground for children attending York's elementary schools, from 9 to 12 each morning. Donkey rides, swings, seesaws, sand heaps and games were all provided. In 1908 a garden party for the children of the Hungate area of the city took place in the park. This was the start of what would become York's biggest public park, now six acres of land.

The Pavilion in the garden was also used for outside events such as

Homestead carousel 1904 (Joseph Rowntree Foundation)

Homestead Park donkey rides 1904 (Joseph Rowntree Foundation)

Seesaws at Homestead 1904 (Joseph Rowntree Foundation)

a weekend lecture school in 1908, with lectures on modern science, socialism and Christian ethics, and Hebrew reformation. Tickets were 2s 6d.

During the First World War while Seebohm Rowntree was away working with the Friends Ambulance Unit, his wife, Lydia, sent a letter to him, dated 28th November 1916, describing the Zeppelin scare at the Homestead.

Dearest One

Last night we had a Zepp warning about 9.30pm. The maids went onto the nursery verandah and the wretched thing was upon us before we knew. It came so quietly that there was only time to snatch Doo [youngest son Julian aged 5] and go down to the passage by the dining room door – it was evidently making for the Cocoa-works. Our one searchlight was on it most of the time, and the gun going for all it was worth. We put Doo to bed but in half an hour we heard another one in the distance. I went to put a light and some rugs in our junk hole, telling the others to follow with Doo. It was too late. I stood at the door and watched, it was coming from the Mount but in the Waterworks direction. The gun was splendid, it hit more than once and seemed to turn turtle. There were enormous cheers from the crowds which made one feel awfully bad. Then they came and told us it had been brought down. There was a great rush of motor cars down the Skelton [now Shipton] Road, and one big military van evidently to take charge of the Zepp crew.

After this we heard bombs in the distance again. I decided it would be well to go to our little hut. We covered Doo right over his head in my Jaeger dressing gown and got him across the garden quite safely. By this time I had fallen down some frost-covered steps and sprained my ankle, but the girls were splendid. They flew back to the house and got cups and boiling water and we had a cosy cup of tea. When all was quiet at 2.30 am we came back. We sat up in the nursery till the lights went up at 3am, and then with good hot water bottles went off to bed.

My ankle is bruised and swollen but I shall be quite spry before your return. Doo is no worse for his midnight adventure. I trust they did not come to you and you are enjoying life.

Dearest Love
Thine SH [Sweetheart]

In 1935, whilst living at the Homestead, Seebohm directed his second survey of poverty in York, which resulted in his book 'Poverty and Progress'. He wrote the work in his library, employing two typists and three researchers. In 1936 he sold the property to the Joseph Rowntree Village Trust at its land value of £12,000, with the proviso that the gardens be maintained as a park for the public. His son Peter, director of Rowntree's until 1964, rented the house from 1936 to 1978. During the Second World War, the Homestead and park were severely damaged in the Blitz on York in April 1942. The greenhouses, monkey house and aviary were all destroyed and the rock garden left in a poor condition. The same year, Peter's wife Bessie died aged 30, and Seebohm's wife, Lydia, died in 1944. Seebohm left York and he died in 1954.

Beverley House, which was next door to the Homestead, had been owned by Colonel Reginald Frank Morris in 1902 and later sold to Thomas Appleton, general manager at Rowntree's. After the Second World War, the Rowntrees purchased the house, added two wings, and incorporated it into the office complex for the three Joseph Rowntree Trusts.

Bill Sessions

Seebohm Rowntree's children, Peter, Joseph Seebohm and Mary 1907
(Joseph Rowntree Foundation)

became a trustee of the Joseph Rowntree Village Trust in 1947 when I was in my early 30s. During the war

Joseph Rowntree with Nancy Astor (First female MP) July 1920 (Joseph Rowntree Foundation)

I worked in London helping to get elderly people out from the horror of living alone with the bombs raging down, and keep them away from the bombs and later the even more dreadful flying bombs and rockets. Thoughts began to turn towards the reconstruction after the war, rebuilding a better Britain and Seebohm Rowntree was asked to chair the Nuffield Foundation to look into the future needs of old people. He said, 'I'd like to find somebody reliable who could do a survey of the almshouses of York'. I did Appendix 13, 'The Almshouses of York', of this Nuffield report. I became known to Seebohm through this. The three senior Rowntrees, Seebohm, John Stephenson Rowntree [Joseph's brother] *from Scarborough, and Arnold Rowntree,* [John's son] *each chaired one of the three Rowntree trusts. To my surprise I was invited to be a trustee of the Village Trust which in 1959 became the Joseph Rowntree Memorial Housing Trust, and in later years the Joseph Rowntree Foundation. I was a trustee for 43 years. Quakers, I suppose, are a fairly close-knit friendly community. If somebody is down on their luck or needing help* [such as] *transport to the hospital, and they can offer it, it would be out of religious concern than any rigid rules.*

In 1978 when Peter Rowntree and his family left the Homestead, the house became the head office of Rowntree Mackintosh, following the merger of the two firms. The office moved back to Haxby Road in 1989

Bill Sessions 2011 (Van Wilson)

when Nestlé took over the firm, and in 1990 the Homestead and Beverley House became the offices of the Joseph Rowntree Foundation, an amalgamation of all the previous Rowntree's Trusts. (The Foundation had been originally established to administer Joseph Rowntree's model village of New Earswick).

The Homestead grounds soon became well-loved by families from near and far. Sheila Goater visited as a girl before the Second World War.

It was a great fascination, nice swings and slides, all covered in, it had a roof over it. There was that awful roundabout that we used to call the Yorkshire Bumps, those things that go round and up and down, and you feel sick.

It always had a pond with goldfish. You could walk all round it, there was a wooden bridge. And there were monkeys. I remember one of my cousins came, she had a coat with a fur wrist band, and this monkey put its hand out to get hold of the fur. When my children were small the Homestead was used by groups for sports days, on the lawns in the Homestead itself.

Homestead House 1932 (*Joseph Rowntree Foundation*)

Marion Tweedy also recalls the monkeys,

> *I remember a boy being bitten and my father running to the doctor's with him. There was a wooden thing to keep you away from them but you know what boys are like.*

Derek Metcalfe went to the Homestead as a child after the war.

> *My grandma took me, I must have been five or six. We'd walk down to the Homestead along the river. They'd give you a beanbag, I don't think ball games were permitted. I remember on the left hand side an enormous bomb hole.*

Margaret Arnold went to Ebor School in Clifton.

> *I can remember doing something in the Homestead, like dancing and playing the piano there, a children's school play. And the scouts used to have a big fair in the Homestead.*

Doug Heald recalls

going fruit picking in the Homestead to supplement my mother's income in the holidays. Redcurrant picking or blackcurrant. Used to get lots of families doing that. You'd get so much a punnet. [Part of the park had been a market garden, the Clifton Fruit Company run by Peter Rowntree until 1960].

Pauline Wright

used to go up every afternoon with my mother. I remember buying the most wonderful tomatoes, warm, out of the greenhouse. I've never had tomatoes that tasted the same since.

Charles Alcorn came to the Homestead in 1970.

I was head gardener and garden manager for 24 years. When I first came it was basic, money hadn't been spent on the gardens. The glasshouses were very dilapidated. The playground was a bit old fashioned. The plantings were not very good and everything needed updating. Fortunately I had a very good superior who made money available for modernising the park. Money was available for replanting which was badly needed.

The headquarters were in Beverley House and about six office staff. There wasn't a tennis court below Beverley House. It was all blackcurrants and vegetables. We decided that was not economical. We did away with that. The whole area was grassed down and gradually we planted trees. It was a nice picnic area. We managed to get the money to put really good fencing right round the whole property, from Beverley House down to the Ings, and up the other side, between us and the youth hostel. We couldn't do much in the lower fields because of flooding each winter. The playground had iron seesaws, iron roundabouts, rusted and very poor, and in this day and age it would be condemned. We introduced modern equipment and made it one of the best play parks in York.

The glasshouses were old lean-to ones and had been a monkey house. We put up very good modern glasshouses. A tractor shed was put up below Beverley House and a few years later somebody fired it and burned it down. But we decided to put up a bigger one next to the playground. Next to the glasshouses was the men's area for their meals, an old shed with brick flooring, very basic, and the money was made available to update this, put in a shower unit and areas for cooking. Opposite the office for garden staff was the pavilion [designed by Fred Rowntree]. *This was initially used by the WI* [Women's Institute] *and other organisations for their weekly meetings. This went on for a few years and then it was decided to finish with hiring it out and turn it into offices. The staff were growing and they needed more accommodation. There wasn't a car park at Shipton Road initially and there was a car park at Water End, but it was abused by people running their cars into the herbaceous border.* [Shipton Road car park was constructed in the late 1970s].

What is the Homestead offices now, was Peter Rowntree's house. And we maintained the grounds while he was in residence. We had roughly 18 to 20 gardeners, but not all occupied at the Homestead. There were so many maintaining New Earswick and various properties at Hull, Beverley, Thornton Dale, Poppleton Road, Acomb.

A lot of it is completely altered, new plants and beds put in. On the far side of the park there was no path leading down to the playground. It was a matter of looking at what there was, a lot of little beds dotted about the place, doing away with them and making one big planted area. I had a very free hand in planning and choosing and maintaining, which made it very interesting and rewarding.

In many instances I wanted trees and bushes and shrubs that weren't just ordinary. I would have to travel round quite a lot of nurseries looking. There was one particular one that supplied good trees and that was Daleside Nursery at Killinghall. The idea is that there is something of interest all the year. Fashions change, now you see plants growing that wouldn't have been considered 20 years ago. At one time it was all bedding, rows and rows of geraniums, but those are changing, people are using grasses, lavenders, ferns and all sorts to give a variety of foliage. There's a lot of interest in hucara, a red leaved herbaceous plant.

Today there are over 46,000 bedding plants.

Charles Alcorn, Garden manager
(Joseph Rowntree Foundation)

People are looking all the time at something new and trying it. At one time we'd got nearly 100 different varieties of hebes, and we lost 80 per cent of those within a couple of years because we were getting much severer winters. It was trial and error. You can have a lot of competition from tree roots. You get a very dry summer and the tree roots are sucking all the moisture out of the ground. We planted hundreds and hundreds of trees. Not just here but in various places.

Security was a big problem at one time. Used to get a tremendous amount of vandalism. We had to get a security man in to keep an eye on people. You'd lose a lot of plants, get a lot broken, just for no reason at all.

We had quite a few girls working for us over the years. But mostly men. *Maybe just five per cent would be girls, but I always found them very good. The trouble is that people are not so interested in horticulture or gardening now. They look at other jobs and it's difficult to get trained staff in horticulture.*

I used to do a lot of judging at flower shows and I gave a lot of talks for various organisations. It got a little bit out of hand. At one time, we had students from Askham Bryan and various groups to be taken round, a lot of places were asking you for advice. There's a little hut in the playground, it's not exactly a café. One of the York firms has the right to sell ice-cream and soft drinks during the summer. The pavilion at one time supplied teas and so forth, various organisations used to run it. People would come and have fêtes, advertising them at the gate and they would have more or less the use of the park.

The pond is still there with the fish. At one time it was all planted up with alpines and got badly abused. After you get a few hundred feet tramping over plants, they disappear. It is a big job draining the pond. There might be as much as a foot of silt, and this has all got to be barrowed out and taken away. All the fish have got to be caught and put into containers then reintroduced into the pond.

There's not much of a rose garden. It's not a suitable soil for roses. There have been various areas tried, I used to propagate them. Then we grew Christmas trees as well. And we propagated a lot of our shrubs.

Planting up time is a very busy time, probably about May and early June. And then in the autumn when you're pulling everything out and getting the planting in again. If you get a very hot season when the grass has not grown so much, things quieten down. If it's a very snowy winter, there's not much that can be done outside except clearing the snow.

Although I was garden manager, I found it much better to be on the site with the men. They saw if I was willing to muck in and do the jobs that they were doing, there was no reason that they couldn't do anything. The use of machinery does affect you. I had what they call trouble in your wrists, with the continuing vibration. You can easily have an accident. You can be pulling out trees with a tractor and suddenly the cable snaps and whips and somebody gets it across them. You can have men up a tree sawing the tree down and something goes wrong and a branch comes down and hits somebody or the power saw whips round their wrist. At times it can be stressful and you've got quite a number of jobs happening at the same time. But it's all enjoyable. Planning things and getting them planted up and seeing the development of them was interesting.

In the summer months you can get a few hundred people in a day. You could hardly find a place to sit at one time. At one time it was a quiet road but now the noise of traffic is continuous.

Cherry Tree Avenue, Homestead (Joseph Rowntree Foundation)

71

The Trust also owns 36 and 38 Water End for the Homestead gardeners. In Cherry Avenue, eleven trees on either side were planted in 1910 and are now seven metres tall. In October 2004, to celebrate 100 years since Seebohm Rowntree first opened the Homestead to the public, the Joseph Rowntree Foundation had an open day and over 200 children were given free ice creams and donkey rides, and tried out the new play equipment installed.

OUSE LEA

The rear of the Homestead now has a car park on Shipton Road. Next door is Ouse Lea which was originally one house. In 1891 George Crombie, who owned a business in Stonegate, lived there and owned one of the six telephones in Clifton, number 40.

Dr Peter MacDonald, physician and surgeon, (who had his practice at 59 Bootham), and his wife Agnes, daughter of Joseph Rowntree and sister of Seebohm, lived at Ouse Lea until he sold the house to the Joseph Rowntree Memorial Trust in 1961, after Agnes's death in 1960. It became part of the Homestead site but was later sold, because of council pressure and the need for more housing. The Trust still assists with maintenance of the gardens but the site now has 31 town houses, apartments and maisonettes, the earliest built in 1965.

The York Stained Glass Trust is also based in Ouse Lea and work is being done to establish a Stained Glass centre in St Martin cum Gregory Church in Micklegate.

– Chapter 5 –
ALMSHOUSES

Almshouses were first recorded in Britain in the 10th century and were usually founded by the local nobility to house and provide for the poor. The giving of alms became the means of survival for those on the margins of society. The name derives from the Greek for compassion. At one time there were 50 almshouses in the city of York. Only a dozen remain today. There are three located in Clifton, and another two in Bootham.

Carole Smith at Wandesford House
(Carole Smith)

WANDESFORD HOUSE

Wandesford House is next to Bootham School and was founded in 1739 to house 'ten poor widows'. There is a bust of the benefactress Mary Wandesford above the front door. She died in 1725, bequeathing an estate at Brompton-upon-Swale, near Richmond, with a mortgage of £1200 and funds in trust 'for the use and benefit of ten poor gentlewomen, who were members of the established church, were never married, who shall retire from the hurry and noise of the world into a house of Protestant retirement'. The property was built in 1743. It remained largely unaltered until the roof was replaced in 1927. In 1947 there were ten residents and the property was valued at £3750. Eight years later, in 1954, it became a Grade II* listed building.

Carole Smith is the current Clerk to the Trustees.

The house was for women to come and retire from the world. This went down rather badly with the family and they took it to the Court of Chancery. The Court upheld the will [of Mary Wandesford] *but said that the minimum age admission was 50. They couldn't be young women coming in and becoming nuns. They bought this house, the wall at the bottom is next to Bootham tennis courts. There was also an orchard, that was let out to get some income for the house. In the back garden here there were outside privies. It was called the 'Old Maids' Hospital' for a long time. There was a farm which used to be part of the endowment. It was sold in the 1950s because there wasn't any money for upkeep.*

The ladies are not tenants, they are beneficiaries of the charity, they're licensees in terms of the contract. The Almshouses Association encourages the almshouses to make it as easy as possible to stay in their homes, so they have carers coming in. The majority now are mid to late 80s or over 90. We have a duty of care. If anything happens we deal with it.

The house has been re-designed. It was originally for ten women, each with a downstairs sitting room and an upstairs bedroom, and a common room for all. In 1947 there was this survey of almshouses, [by Bill Sessions] *of poverty and old age. The government began to put money towards upgrading this kind of establishment. So it's split up into two bedsits and four flats. A common room was created and upstairs there's a chapel which is still in use. We have a chaplain comes once a month to give communion.*

There's never been staff, but there's always been a porteress, like a concierge, who isn't meant to do anything except manage the house, keep an eye on it and report to the clerk about leaks and damage, repair jobs needing doing and that kind of thing. You get a lot of light, and good sized rooms compared with lots of modern flats. There's a fireplace in the common room and the possibility of having coal fires in the winter. You have ventilation shafts. The roof is absolutely amazing, it's huge. The chapel has been painted a nice stone colour. We were left some money by the Dean's wife to furbish the house. So we painted the chapel and did various other things.

There's always been the requirement to be a member of the church. That's true of all almshouses. In the past it was probably 'people of good character', because they were regarded as godly houses, the old name for them is Maison Dieu, God House.

The caretaker is a very involving kind of person. It's always been a happy house but it's got a very different atmosphere. It doesn't smell like an institution. They have a chapel fund and they buy the flowers from that. The sitting room has become a place where, if you feel like a conversation or chat, you come and sit here and read the paper, and people are coming and going. If the parrot's in, [which belongs to the caretaker], *people automatically talk to the parrot.*

I think their lives used to be controlled [which is obviously not the case today]. *People who are poor are always controlled by people who are not poor. In the past if you got ill, you had to go to the workhouse or the Public Assistance House or the asylum. People in almshouses have generally been treated with compassion. Nevertheless I think it's always been the great and the good who would become trustees. There's a residents' party once a year and we invite all the people who've helped us during the year. But it's not a group that needs help, it could be seen as patronising. There's a great danger in offering people who are getting older, assistance with this, that and the other, or a party or a trip out, having to go because somebody else has organised it. We have a residents' meeting once a year, to talk about things that have happened. And we've got a woman chair who is very good at keeping the atmosphere relaxed and involving, engaging and inclusive.*

Ingram's Hospital (*Christine Kyriacou*)

INGRAM'S HOSPITAL

Ingram's Hospital was built in Bootham, in about 1640, endowed by the will of Sir Arthur Ingram, a landowner and politician. It has a very distinctive two storey building with small doorways, which contained five sets of rooms, providing accommodation for 'ten poor widows'. The building was dominated by a low central tower over a chapel and caretakers' rooms. The decorative central doorway of about 1190 is said to have been brought from Holy Trinity Priory after the Dissolution. The owners of Ingram's estate at Temple Newsam paid £50 yearly to support the charity, plus £6 13s. 4d. for the reading of prayers in the chapel. In the 1947 survey, each flat had a living room with open fireplace, staircase leading to 'an unheated bedroom, a wash house with sink and cold tap but no bath'. At this time there were 11 residents and the value of the property was £2,500. In 1957 the York Charity Trustees agreed to let a private philanthropic concern, Ings Trust, take over the hospital in return for a gift of land on which a new hospital was to be built. The exterior of Ingram's has been preserved and the interior divided into four flats.

FOTHERGIL HOMES

The Thomas Fothergil 'Homes for Working Men and Women' in Avenue Road, Clifton, were built in 1935 with resident management staff and activities laid on for residents. The charity was regulated by a scheme in 1936 which fixed the number at ten 'poor working people of good character, ten years resident in York', made up of five men and five women.

The homes are built of brick in an L shape. Each has a bedroom, living room, bathroom and wc, and kitchen. Carole Smith explains

Fothergil Homes were originally built to designs by Ward and Leckenby. They were extended around 1957 into the back of the property belonging to JB Morrell (Burton Croft in Burton Stone Lane) and again at various times from the 1960s onwards, and are now the largest almshouses in York with accommodation for up to 60 people.

COLTON'S HOSPITAL

Thomas and Mary Colton's Hospital, at the corner of Rougier Street and Tanner Row, was founded in 1717, with houses for 'eight poor women'. The houses were acquired by the corporation for £2,500, because of street widening, and the Hospital moved to Shipton Street, off Burton Stone Lane. Eight one-storey brick almshouses were built, with four more added in 1932. The Coltons were Presbyterian dissenters and preference was originally given to Unitarians in the selection of the 12 residents.
The hospital was endowed with lands at Thorpe Willoughby and Cawood, providing an annual fund of £50, until the land was sold in 1956, and the trustees held £1,794 in stock.

Colton's Hospital (Van Wilson)

Carole Smith explains

Dr Colton was Lady Hewley's chaplain. [Lady Sarah Hewley was the wife of Sir John Hewley, MP for York, in 1678-1681. She had made Thomas Colton, minister of St Luke's Church on Burton Stone Lane, her executor]. *She founded Lady Hewley's Cottages* [in St Saviourgate] *in 1700. At the moment the trustees of Colton's are the same trustees of the Unitarian Chapel in St Saviourgate, which was built with Lady Hewley's money. Colton's has never had a problem with Unitarianism and the endless wrangling that went on in the 19th century. The trustees take much more interest, and make themselves available for getting phone calls if work needs doing.*

The trustees or landlords of the Hospital are part of the charity which is endowed by the York Unitarian Church. Beneficiaries of the trust have to be single ladies aged 55 or over. The twelve cottages are centered around a small green. Each one has a little piece of garden, and inside a sitting room, bedroom, kitchen and bathroom. A gardener looks after the grounds, including the trees and shrubs which surround the lawns. In the York Unitarian newsletter, one of the trustees, Marta Hardy, recounts a problem when a swarm of bees took up residence at Colton's Hospital.

I didn't want Pest Control to come in with their poisons. It took me the better part of a day to locate a beekeeper who was able to come and retrieve the swarm. She enquired rather anxiously on the phone whether I was certain it was bees, since once she had driven two hours to find a swarm of wasps awaiting her. She drove in from Wilberfoss and we watched fascinated as she donned her beekeepers' gear, lit a little smoke machine, and set an ordinary cardboard box below where the bees were churning around buzzing. Then she drew out, of all things, a goose's wing, and very gently began brushing the bees into the box. Quite soon bees that were flying about started heading for the box, which meant that the Queen was captured. When practically all of the bees were in the box, the beekeeper just put a blanket over the top, packed up her things, and went home.

JOHN BURRILL HOMES

The John Burrill Homes in Water End, Clifton, were built in 1931 and comprise seven single storey cottages, each with several rooms, designed by Ward and Leckenby. John Burrill was a director of Border's grocers in Coney Street and a governor of Bootham Park. He died in July 1924 and left money to provide a home for widows of men in the grocery trade. He had been involved in Clifton for many years and was the treasurer of Clifton Conservative Association in 1886.

The cottages have stone mullioned bay windows which look onto a spacious green, with trees and flower beds, and a stone sundial.

Burrill Homes in snow (Derek Metcalfe)

Derek Metcalfe

used to be a trustee of the almshouses, of John Burrill's. Ellison's Terrace was where John Burrill used to live, in the farmhouse with his sisters, he was a single gentleman and he owned Border's near the Mansion House down Coney Street. He made his money there and when he died, he left most of his money to have the John Burrill Homes built.

Lucy Staples lives near the Homes and often visits friends there.

There is a couple in there, caretakers, and they're very good. They keep the paths clear and see to the residents.

There are allotments, gardens at the back which each had a bit of ground to grow their own vegetables. My husband and I had one for a while but he wasn't a very keen gardener. It was for vegetables and fruit. One lady has raspberries galore. There is a big space

Burrill Homes Sundial (*Christine Kyriacou*)

behind, which I think originally was to build some more cottages but there's no access to it.

Mary Morris lives there.

They were for widows of the grocery trade. Then it quickly became that there weren't enough and they opened it up [to others]. *The architect was marvellous, and in actual fact it's a listed building now.* [The houses became Grade II listed in 1997]. *It looks a lot older than it is. In Clifton Parish Church, going up to the belfrey, on the door it says, 'This is in memory of John Burrill'.*

It's lovely, we don't hear the traffic here. We used to get vibrations from the sugar beet lorries going past but we don't get that now of course, which is an added bonus. The statue in the centre, it's Ruth in the Bible, and it was originally a sundial. All the six cottages are totally individual. The caretakers live at number 4. They are very good. It's an independent organisation, doesn't belong to anyone else. It seems to run pretty well. We don't see the five trustees very often. They do come round at Christmas.

– Chapter 6 –

BURTON STONE LANE

The Burton Stone Lane area of York, although obviously part of Clifton, is also a self contained community. Burton Stone Lane is the longest street in Clifton, and one of the longest in York, with houses numbered up to 408. Stretching down from the Burton Stone Inn, it goes beyond the junction with Crichton Avenue, which leads to Kingsway and Burdike, and on to the allotments beside the railway line at Wigginton Road. But 150 years ago this was a peaceful semi-rural part of the city and not the busy, bustling area it is today. The map of 1849 shows Burton Lane, as it then was, as open land, with a few houses and two distinguishing landmarks, one of which remains and one which has gone. The latter is the Lady or

Burton Stone Lane windmill 1860

Clifton Windmill, at the north end of the Lane, which stood there from the late 14th century. In 1374 it was owned by John de Roucliff, William Ingleby owned it by 1442, and, in 1721, it became the property of William Robinson who owned much of Clifton. 'Robert Dent's, later John Knight's, Windmill' was advertised for sale in Clifton in the York Courant in February 1807. The first appearance on a map is in 1772 and the last record of it being operational was in 1852. It was still standing in 1870 but disappeared soon after.

The other landmark is the Burton Stone, at the Clifton end of the

Lane, which is now outside the Burton Stone Inn, enclosed by railings. C B Knight explains that, 'In 1604 there was a violent outbreak of plague in the city and 3,512 persons are said to have died. Stone crosses were erected on the main high roads approaching the city, where the country people exposed their provisions for sale without entering the city. The Burton Stone was the base of one of these crosses'. The Royal Commission on Historical Monuments states that Mother Shipton's Stone on the corner of Rawcliffe Lane (of which there is no longer any trace) may have been part of the cross.

The chapel and hospital of St Mary Magdalene stood at this site, on what was then Chapel Lane, in medieval times. It was the property of the king in 1227 and was later given to the order of Dominican Friars. The hospital was suppressed by Henry VIII and passed to the Burtons, a prominent York family. The chapel and hospital had gone by the early 18th century. Today there are blocks of flats in the Lane with the names of Magdalene House and Mawdlin House.

The Burton Stone Inn was first mentioned in records in 1828, and was originally the Plough. The pub changed its name because of the stone which stood nearer to the road. The Inn was demolished and rebuilt in 1896. Hugh Murray states that, 'During the building work the stone was re-sited into an alcove in the new boundary wall. The council agreed in March 1899 to pay the Tadcaster Tower Brewery, the pub's owners, one penny a year rent'. As well as catering for local people, it was a favourite haunt during the Second World War, of RAF personnel who were based at airfields around the city. The film actor Patrick (Pat) Kinsella was one of these, whose party piece was to recite Shakespeare with a pint of beer balanced on his head, then stand up without spilling a drop. He was sadly killed in action in 1942. The clock in the pub at that time was in the shape of a woman and it became hard to tell the right time as the airmen were always moving the pointers around. In the 1960s the Inn had a social club which held its first walk on Boxing Day 1967.

Burton Stone Inn demolished 1896 (Hugh Murray)

Doug Heald recalls it in the late '50s,

> *The Burton Stone became a local in my late teens. It was different rooms, smoke, lounge, tap room and music room. On a Friday night there was this guy banging away on the piano, we'd get a song going and he just played along with it. We had some wonderful times in the music lounge.*

By the beginning of the 20th century, Burton Lane, as it was then called, was the site of two quite substantial properties, Burton Croft and Burton Grange.

Road sign (Christine Kyriacou)

The Burton Stone 2011 *(Christine Kyriacou)*

BURTON CROFT

In 1907 it became the home of John Bowes Morrell until his death in 1963. Described as 'York's greatest benefactor', he was twice Lord Mayor of York, an Honorary Freeman of the city, Rowntree's youngest ever director, instrumental in the foundation of the University of York and its Pro-Chancellor. He instigated the opening of the Castle Museum, was co-founder of York Civic Trust and founder of York Conservation Trust.

J B Morrell was held in great esteem in the city. He was the author of several books on York, and when he first stood for the city council in 1905, he suggested the idea of a bridge to link Clifton with Poppleton Road. It would be nearly sixty years until that became a reality. He became chairman of the Westminster Press group who later owned the Yorkshire Evening Press, and was a collector of pictures, silver and china, with which he filled the house. He was also a lover of books and spent much of his time in his large library. Described as a generous and hospitable man, he regularly entertained not only his own friends and colleagues, but also Bootham schoolboys who often came for Sunday lunch. In the 1950s, at the age of 77, he embarked on a 10,000 mile ten-day tour of America to promote York's Festival of the Arts.

Lena Mills recalls that members of Clifton Methodist Church sometimes visited the house.

We used to go and sing carols there on Christmas Eve. He always came out with a big box of chocolates for us. And he let us use his tennis courts. He had a swimming pool there for his daughter too. It's a shame they pulled it down and they built those flats.

During the Second World War, the house was used as a centre for blood donors. In the late 1960s it was a Methodist hostel for overseas students. In more recent years, it became a home for the elderly but, when that closed, squatters moved in. In 2004, the decision was made to demolish the house. Many people had hoped that the Victorian building could be rescued and a petition was presented to the council, but it was to no avail. Today the house has been replaced by flats named Burton Croft and Burton Court.

BURTON GRANGE

Burton Grange was situated a little further down the Lane from Burton Croft. Opposite the house was a cricket ground and pavilion, used occasionally by St Peter's School. Built in the early 19th century, the Grange was first mentioned in local newspapers when it was advertised for sale in April 1840, and then 'to let' in January 1860. At the turn of the century it was owned by Charlotte Wharton, daughter of the Rev William Wharton of Gilling. She died in 1909. Eliza Kirby remembers the house,

Burton Stone Lane was all trees from Avenue Road past J B Morrell's house. And then there was a big house, Miss Wharton's. It was very dark and lonely down there and it wasn't considered very nice for young girls to be out on their own down that lane.

After Miss Wharton's death, the Burton Grange estate was auctioned in six lots on 4th November 1910. The estate comprised 31 acres, 1 rood and 17 perches, and the auction took place at Harker's Hotel in St Helen's Square.

The house itself was a sizeable one, with seven bedrooms and three servants' bedrooms. Downstairs there was a conservatory, breakfast room, dining room, drawing room, with the housekeeper's room, kitchen, butler's pantry, servants' hall, boot room, store room, scullery, larder, dairy and wine cellar. The outbuildings consisted of two coach houses, a three stall stable with loft, loose box, harness room, laundry, potting shed, stick house, cow house, manure house, hen house, wood built Dutch barn and shed. Nearby were a vinery and greenhouse. The lot also included the five-roomed gardener's cottage. The final lot, Number Six, comprised two cottages with stables, outbuildings and gardens, plus two grass paddocks which fronted Clifton, and two grass fields. There was a small dike which joined the Burdike in Water Lane through a culvert, though at times the lower field did get flooded.

With the purchase of Lot Six came the common rights (for grazing animals) on Clifton Ings. All the fields were surrounded by hawthorn hedges except the boundary on Miss Wharton's pastures. The sale particulars stated that the property was 'a quarter of an hour's walk of the Minster, and within reach of St Peter's Grammar School, good ladies' schools, business establishments, and three packs of hounds'!

The Burton Grange estate took up all the land from the back of Burton Croft, up to the main road between Avenue Terrace and Water Lane, and stretched as far as Cromer Street, near the bottom of Burton Stone Lane. Photographs of Burton Lane in 1910, show it to be a leafy rural scene, and the Burton Lane District children's carnival was held that year. Within a few years of the sale of the house and the other plots of land, which were described as ripe for building, the First World War intervened. Most large houses tended to be requisitioned for hospitals or to billet troops. Burton Grange was no exception, and troops occupied much of the house.

After the war, the house was renovated to be used as accommodation for the boarders of York College for Girls in Low Petergate, from 1919 to the early 1930s. Eleanor R was a pupil there. Her very descriptive memories were sent to the late Jennifer Kaner.

About mid-afternoon one day towards the middle of September 1923, a tall lady nearing fifty, carrying a large handbag and accompanied by a chubby ten year old girl, alighted from the bus in Burton Stone Lane. They made their way on the north side eastwards, past Burton Croft, the home of J B Morrell, to Burton Grange. Up the long drive, bordered by trees and a high walled ginnel known as Love Lane, they noticed at the turn of the drive, the tallest and largest tree that the child had ever seen. Two or three years later she would be still more amazed when from its top she gazed down at the rooftops beneath her. It was forty feet or more in height, a glorious copper beech of great girth and spread, home of countless generations of owls and squirrels. In spring the ground below would become a wonderland of beauty with a vast carpet of mauve and white crocuses, in autumn a happy hunting ground for beech nuts.

At the top of the drive stood Miss Davies, in cream buttoned-up blouse, and almost ankle length dark skirt, cheerful and welcoming, ex-secretary to Lady Wilberforce Bell, and an endless source of quirky and whimsical tales about the Bell household. Miss Davies and my mother went into the drawing room and I was left sitting in the hall where there were runs of carpet on a polished floor, a couple of hard chairs, a plant on a round table, and an elegant staircase, of an excellent slope, as I would find out later, for descending at speed on a teatray. I was taken into the common room with its large basket chairs, pink tiled fireplace and big bay windows. The dining room had French windows opening onto the lawns, and through a passage were narrow, twisty back stairs which the girls and the maids would normally use. Burton Grange, unified generally at ground floor level, was upstairs a thoroughly higgledy piggledy place of front stairs, back stairs and middle stairs with steps up or down into almost every room in the main house.

Burton Lane (later Burton Stone Lane) 1900s

*The gardens always meant more to us than the house. There were
lawns and flowerbeds, a full sized tennis court. There were lots
of good hiding places, behind doorways and among trees, in the
woodshed, in the old stokehole of the hot greenhouse and in the
shrubbery, a rather eerie place concealing up-ended crockets, brought,
we were told, from St Mary's Abbey, which we chose to call gargoyles.
There were great days in winter, walking among the frozen fallen
leaves, and jumping down from the high wall above the espaliers
on to resilient piles of dry foliage. There were just ten of us boarders
in my first term, most of us were clergy daughters, there at reduced
fees. Not until 1925 when numbers had risen to 20, did the new
wing dormitories above the old stables come into use. The climbing
era set in. We began to explore the giant beech tree, to traverse the
now tottering coping stones of the garden wall above the fruit trees,
descending at intervals to sample the season's produce, eternally
hungry as boarding school children always were, and attempting
the more difficult and dangerous trees by the spiky railings which*

bordered the ginnel leading down to the old hockey pitch off Cromer Street.

Much of our exercise consisted in proceeding from place to place in the orderly form of 'crocs'. We crocked one mile to school every morning. We crocked to the shops or Yearsley Baths on Saturdays and church on Sundays. Often this was three times, for the confirmed girls to nearby St Luke's at 8am, for Matins we went to St Olave's, and on Sunday afternoons we trooped to the Minster for evensong and enjoyed the splendid music of the choir with Dr Edward Bairstow at the organ. It was inevitable that so much 'crocking' should lead to misdemeanour. We returned on Sunday mornings from St Olave's by the river path and then a variety of ginnels which had not yet been identified as the subsidiary roads and lanes of the northern Roman suburb. As the croc prepared to turn towards BG, the leaders and two smaller children simply walked on, for the entire length of Clifton Ings and somewhat further, returning in time for tea. I remember the only time we were punished was when some of us had our much-loved yearly visit to the Gala [in Bootham Park] cancelled. We composed the parody, 'Standing one day at the window, weary and worn and sad, For the others had gone to the Gala, we hadn't, and so we were mad'.

Then boys began to materialise. Boothamites, Peterites, and older boys from the Minster Song School. There were clandestine meetings under the trees of the hockey pitch, encounters on the Clifton path and in Love Lane, while on shopping expeditions boys emerged from behind doors and display stalls, and above all from between the book stacks of Edwin Storey's shop in Bootham, opposite to the delicious smells of Britton's grocery where the coffee was roasted in the window. Perhaps the highlight was when one girl's brother, Puffy, led a party of Peterites up the pear tree into his sister's dorm. Miraculously the tree survived the onslaught.

The Burton Grange regime had a threefold structure. Above us were the staff, matron and her assistant, school staff who were resident,

*the cook and laundress. Somewhere beneath, were our good friends
the 'skivs'. Like us they wore a uniform, used the back stairs, had
their own back door, and slept in their own dorm. They got up even
earlier than our rising bell, though unlike our Spartan selves, they
did not take cold baths. They understood we were always hungry, and
would fetch from the local chipper on late summer evenings, fries in
brown paper carriers to be hauled up to the far wing dorm through
the long suffering pear tree. Probably the fry-ups hastened the demise
of the dormitory feasts which were a regular feature of our lives.
I remember in the babies' dorm, by the light of the fire we were
sometimes allowed on the last night of the Christmas term, that one
year we played whist all night.*

*We began to go to concerts and the theatre. One outcome was that
we began to organise ourselves as a common room and purchased
a gramophone and records. I remember not only 'Tea for Two' and
'The Riff Song' but also duets from Il Trovatore and Peter Dawson's
dramatic singing of 'Boots'. On long Sunday evenings we trooped
into the drawing room and Mrs Humphries and Mrs Palmer would
read to us. Mrs Palmer took us at a spanking pace through the entire
output of Anthony Hope* ['The Prisoner of Zenda'], *Ernest Raymond,
Sapper and P C Wren. She also taught us to play bridge.*

*Not only had the wing dormitories been opened in those middle
years but also a large corrugated iron building sited on part of the
extensive vegetable gardens beyond the wing, known as the 'Rec'. A
high echoing place, where for a time we did prep in the evenings.
Freezing in winter, over-hot in summer, with shaky tables and poorly
lit, it possessed an old, large and probably dangerous stove which
nevertheless was ideal for roasting chestnuts.*

*By the end of the '20s our childhood had gone. We no longer used the
swing outside the Rec. We wrote diaries, letters, stories and verses by
reams. Cold baths and dawn rambles were replaced by early piano
practice, and we used the pianos a lot in the evenings. Studies were
contrived out of the old laundry airing room and one of the stables. It*

was beautifully snug in winter. I remember an increase in excursions into the countryside and on the river. Buttercrambe Woods in a real charabanc with separate doors for each row of open seats, where we collected marsh plants. But the economic problems of the end of the '20s had been signalised for us by the drop in price of Walter's Palm Toffee at the Cromer Street corner shop, to a penny a quarter. Then came the closing down of the Misses Gibbs' cake and confectionery shop halfway up Burton Stone Lane. How we had rejoiced when it opened in 1927 and we were introduced to whipped cream walnut and Rowntree's motoring chocolate.

Domestic help shrank in the latter years and the maids' dorm was closed as was the laundry, washing being again sent out. In 1931 Mrs Palmer and her glamorous daughter, who had for a time taught French, had left. In 1933, Burton Grange closed, and by 1935 the house, tree, garden and fields had fallen to the developer, replaced by Lumley Road, Burton Avenue and St Luke's Grove. Only the

Burton Stone Lane, Clifton end 2011 (Christine Kyriacou)

gardener's cottage remained, its walls picturesquely covered with the flowering branches of doubtless climbable trees.

By the 1920s, the Clifton half of Burton Stone Lane had a few more houses, mostly cottages including Burton Lodge and Holt Cottage, opposite Lumley Barracks, St Luke's Parsonage, and St Luke's Church. The terrace which is now numbered 19 to 37 was built on land bought by William Bellerby at the 1836 sale of the De Grey estate. Bellerby had his joiner's yard in the carriageway between numbers 27 and 31. This is still named The Coach Yard. Just before Asylum Lane, next to the Barracks, were the more middle class Burton Villas, whose occupants included the music teachers, Hubert Marchant Haigh and his daughter Lizzie Howarth Haigh. By 1932, work had begun on developing what had been the Burton Grange estate and soon the area was covered in houses. There were still allotments at the end of the Lane, but the small farms had gone, except for one belonging to Lancelot Cussins, situated beyond Cromer Street. Eliza Kirby recalls this farm.

We lived in Cromer Street. Cussins's had a little farm at the bottom of Burton Stone Lane. They had one daughter, Angie, she'd come round lugging a great can of milk. And they had a pint measure. You'd go to the door with the milk basin and she would measure out whatever you took. She didn't stand talking. If her mother caught her talking to anybody, poor Angie got into trouble.

In 1900 the Burton Lane Adult School and Social Club opened in new premises in Falsgrave Crescent. The Adult Schools were founded in the 1850s by Quakers to offer education for working men but were in decline by the 1920s. The building was used for services of the New Lendal Congregational Church before the church on Burton Stone Lane was built in 1935 (and demolished in 1995). The centre was used as a British Restaurant during the Second World War. Today York Travellers' Trust and York Racial Equality Network are based in Falsgrave Crescent.

Cromer Street had been built in the early years of the 20th century, with Surtees Street, Garth Terrace, Horner Street, Ratcliffe Street, Glencoe Street

Burton Stone Lane Adult School (Van Wilson)

and Shipton Street, and smaller terraced streets leading down to the railway. The development was the work of Surtees Hornby of Falsgrave, Scarborough.

There were many shops on these streets, with several grocers, fried fish dealers, butchers, bakers, greengrocers, off licences, a hairdresser's and a watchmaker's. The Corner House pub opened in 1937 to serve the new community. It was a popular venue which provided live music for several decades.

Following the Second World War, there was more housing. But the allotments at the Rowntree Bridge end of the lane had been very important for food.

Gill May's

Gran and Granddad lived on Burton Stone Lane when I was young.

*I did go a lot as a kid. They lived at the bottom end, [number 293].
Granddad used to take me to school. He had a carrier bike, I'd sit
in the front of it. He had an allotment there, down near the railway
lines. He kept pigs. I remember running around after these little pigs.
He kept hens as well. He'd take the eggs to the incubator, hatch them
out and when they were big enough, they'd go onto the allotment
again. I remember sides of bacon being hung up in the bedroom.
My Granddad worked on the railway. They all came from a farming
area. I guess they had livestock when they first started.*

*They were encouraged to grow vegetables and things. That was
the best way for them to get food. I used to pick peas and then
we'd go back to Gran's and shell them. Granddad would grow
chrysanthemums, show them, and win prizes. They'd grow vegetables
and he won prizes for that as well.*

Pauline Wright was born in 1935 and has lived for much of her life in the
Burton Stone Lane area.

*I was born in Horton Road, off Ratcliffe Street, quite close to the
railway. There was houses at one side and fields at the other. My
parents bought that house because it was near Rowntree's and they
could easily walk there. On the corner of nearly every street there
was a shop of some sort. There was Coupe's on the corner of Cromer
Street that became the post office when Scarborough Terrace post
office closed. There was a butcher's and a greengrocer's, Harrison's,
now a Chinese takeaway. On the corner of Surtees Street there was
a general hardware shop, Hutchinson's, then the Thrift general
store. On the corner of Garth Terrace there was Evans who repaired
bicycles. Then it became the sewing and machine knitting shop and
that closed down, it's now a pizza place. There was Walter Willson's
grocery store. On the corner of Horner Street there was Joe's fish
shop, who sold wet fish and then it became the Thrift butcher's shop.
On the other corner was Scaife's grocery shop. It was a lovely shop
because he roasted his own coffee and ground it.*

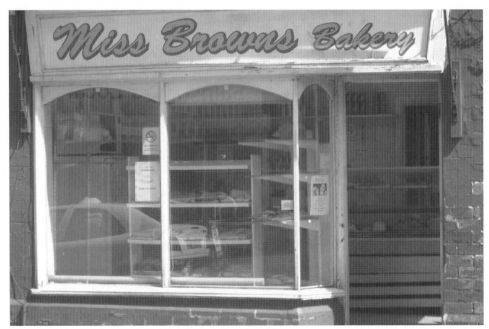

Miss Brown's Bakery 2011 (Van Wilson)

There was Brown's bakery and it is still Miss Brown's bakery, they've just kept the name because it was such a popular shop. You could smell the bread being cooked. There was a haberdasher's and draper's shop on the other corner of Ratcliffe Street. You tended to go to the ones you knew. During the war you had to, because it was rationed and you had to register with a shop and they got your supplies. In Hudson Street that used to be the Co-op, then it became a painter and decorator's. I remember our Co-op number, used to quote it to get our 'divi'. [Dividend number]. *I would go there from six or so. Mother would say, "Now come straight back". You didn't fear, even though it was wartime. We must have spent time swapping things. We could drink Camp Coffee, and I liked coffee, so they'd maybe save some of their tea rations and swap them.*

The radio was very important, especially during the war with the news. I remember my father having a map and showing me where they were talking about on the radio.

I loved Children's Hour, and ITMA and Arthur Askey. But if you had young children you stayed at home. Most of the women didn't go out to work. That's one of the biggest changes in society at large, both parents go out to work because of necessity, it's so expensive now. You didn't go out as much. You went to the cinema, you played games and you went to bed early.

I remember my father taking me on the sledge to the bridge and sliding down. We always called it Rowntree's bridge, everybody did. I used to play out with my friends. There wasn't a lot of cars. The bridge from Grosvenor Road into Bridge Lane, over the railway, was a wooden bridge but the sides were glass and when the steam trains went across, the steam and the smoke came through the boards. There were a lot of trains you see, and Rowntree's had their own. They had a halt from Selby, a lot of workers came in to Rowntree's Halt.

Doug Heald was born in Clifton in 1943.

We moved into Burton Stone Lane when I was eight. It was a tree lined street. Across the road was this park which is still there. They had a bowling green and swings and the usual kiddies area. I went to Shipton Street School. It had an overspill in form 11, which went over to New Lendal Chapel which is now a housing development. We used to line up in the school playing grounds and march in line across the road.

I worked for a butcher at 13, a Mr Wandsford, on the corner of Shipton Street and Baker Street. He used to provide the meat all round the district, as far as Rawcliffe. After school I'd go round and clean the shop, scrub the block, scrub the outside with soda water on the flags to get the grease off. On Tuesday I would get the carrier bike out and deliver meat to various places. When I got to 14, he must have thought I was very good. I was getting ten bob a week for three nights and then within a short time, he asked if I would work for five nights and Saturday, for 30 shillings, which I agreed. It was very hard, leaving school and going straight into work until

6 o'clock. On a Saturday morning he asked me to go in at 6.30, to get everything out of the deep freeze and put on display in the shop. There was always a good steak breakfast but that disappeared after a while and became eggs and bacon.

Saturday afternoon was cleaning up time in the shop, cleaning all the knives and the block, taking the sausage machine to pieces, the mincing machine to pieces and just generally cleaning and swilling outside. Wandsford had a smallholding on Burton Stray, and a pony, well a mule, called Peggy. And on a Saturday afternoon he would go out round all the back streets around that area. People would leave out food that they'd thrown out...potato peelings and stale bread and all that would go into a large bin on the pony and trap. Occasionally I would go out with him, picking up a bucket and throwing it into the bins. This would then be rendered down into pig meat. He would have a big boil up on his allotment. He also kept hens so he sold eggs

Shipton Street School. Doug Heald is second from right on second row from front. c1950
(Douglas Heald)

as well. He'd breed his own pigs. It was always full of little events, like the pony breaking loose and running off, or a bin would fall off and the pig swill would be all over the road. He always kept a brush on the back to brush it over. You never knew what was going to happen, especially on trips when we went out with a horse.

Douglas Heald 1953
(Douglas Heald)

I would go and feed the Wandsford pigs and the hens, and of course this horse would be in the field wanting its oats. I remember once going in there and I accidentally left the gate open and by the time I'd put all the oats out for the pony, it was trotting down Wigginton Road and would it hell come back! My concern was, I had to be in school in half an hour, and I was having to run up the opposite direction to York to try and bring this pony back, and each time I got near it, it would run further. It was only good fortune that there was someone coming who was a farmer that we could bring it back this way.

Really it was a form of slave labour, looking back, for the work you did. I was getting up at six o'clock, delivering the papers and then going to feed the pigs before school, and all my Saturdays were taken up. One of the oddest things, he used to ask me to collect the offal from the cattle market, from the abattoir. I would cycle to the cattle market, stand in the doorway which was always awash with red water from the cattle being slaughtered, then you'd get these huge carcases being pulled along rails where they were cleaning them. I would have to wait where this beast had been killed. On this particular Saturday morning, two men brought this basket, very heavy because the offal was in the basket, and they stuck a cow's head on the top. The butcher would use the cow's cheek and every part in mincemeat and sausage-meat. There'd be this whole weight in the front basket of this carrier bike. I managed to mount the bike and I could feel the weight of all the lights, the cow's heart and lungs which would be rendered down into fat and dripping. So the weight was more than I weighed and it was all jellified. It was very hard to steer. I was coming through the heart of York towards Nessgate corner and you had a policeman and he was bringing everyone forward and then for some reason he put up his hand to stop and, as I applied my brakes, the whole lot spilled out. The whole bike tipped over and I went spinning onto the road and disappeared into the screaming crowd.

This cow's head skimmed across the road and all the lights and the gore and everything. The crowd were screaming and I was embarrassed. This policeman on duty managed to get the help of some other policemen, three or four came from nowhere and it was such a strange sight to see all this blood and gore and the bike with its wheels still spinning. When they realised it had been an accident, they started putting the bits into the basket and called, "Who does this belong to?" And sheepishly I came out of the crowd and said, "It's mine sir". And he gave me a little ticking off. I walked all the way down Coney Street but had to hold down the seat. As I got to Lendal, I was so tired and my wrists were hurting that much, I thought, "I've got to get back on the bike". So I mounted the bike, came down Grosvenor Terrace and into Newborough Street and Shipton Street, and as I came round the corner, I was going quite fast, and my boss the butcher, he was there with his apron on and his hand on his hip, smoking one of his Craven A. And I remember shouting, "Mr Wandsford, I won't be able to stop". And as I approached him, I had to steer away and I tried the brakes and the whole bike turned over again and the whole basket, the cow's head bouncing up the wall, everything coming out again. And he was furious. I was apologising and he said, "It's a bloody good job it didn't happen in town". And I never dared to tell him it did!

My mother was in Burton Stone Lane until she died, she'd be 94.

I remember her always having a full house, people would come along for a chat. You did have a community. On summer evenings, you'd get people hanging over the gates talking, catching up on the news, and the kiddies would be around. There was no television, no computers, that's all made the difference.

Doug's mother, Mrs Mabel Heald, worked for Rowntree's for many years as an overlooker and a shop steward. She campaigned for women's rights at the factory, including maternity leave. She also designed a new form of packaging for Black Magic chocolates so that one person packed an entire box rather than one chocolate at a time. She was the first woman to become a member of the Confectionery Board in London. During the Second World War, she was an armaments inspector in the part of Rowntree's which made munitions. She was also a very keen ballroom dancer who would go to the Tower Ballroom in Blackpool, dance until the early hours, go home and go to work in the morning.

Mabel Heald at Rowntree's, on far right (Douglas Heald)

She'd been creative, she brought the sequence pack out at Rowntree's which was the quick packing, quick assortment. She got an award for that, I think it was £50, which was quite a lot of money in those days. She was well thought of at Rowntree's.

Doug recalls another event, the coronation in 1953.

I remember it vividly, at a neighbour's house. It was a cold June day. My father used to go to Clarence Club and they had these walking matches. There'd been a walking match that day, part of the celebrations. This friend of his dressed up as a Zulu, boot polished himself and had some feathers. They'd had a bit to drink and my father brought him home to have a bath. My mother was not too pleased, the bath sides were all boot polish and greasy. In the late afternoon my mother panicked, we had a coal fire, there was lots of smoke coming out of the chimney. She was proud of her house, worried if the fire engines came they would stick the hose down the chimney. She was petrified and she went to the nearest shop and bought the whole stock of salt to draw the soot from the chimney. The idea was, she'd mixed it in a bowl of water and put it on the fire. It was supposed to evaporate and the salt being a rock formation would crystallise and cling to the salt. Eventually the fire did go out. I remember getting a mug full of sweets at school, a coronation mug. It was a very big event.

There continue to be changes in the housing in Burton Stone Lane. The Lumley Working Men's Club at 17 Burton Stone Lane, was converted into flats in 2001. In the same year Lumley Barracks (covered in a separate chapter) had part of its site demolished to make way for 22 houses.

– Chapter 7 –

CHURCHES

CLIFTON PARISH CHURCH

Before 1867, Clifton was divided between the parishes of St Olave, Marygate, and St Michael le Belfrey. In 1859 the first proposals for an Anglican church in the village itself were made. In October 1861, agreement was given and subscriptions began to come in towards a

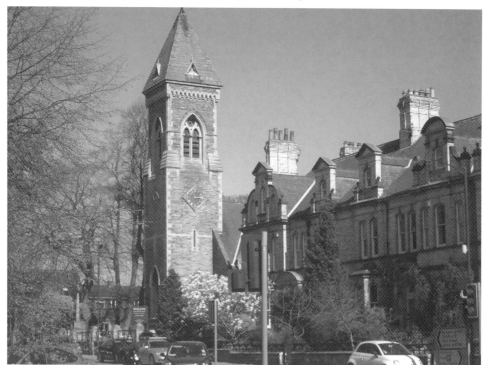

Clifton Parish Church (Van Wilson)

church opposite Clifton Green, which would cover the townships of Clifton and Rawcliffe. The site was a gift from the Patron of the living and Lord of the Manor, Earl de Grey, and after his death, his heirs, the Ladies of the Living, Countess Cowper and Lady Mary Vyner. Lady Mary laid the foundation stone for the new church, St Philip and St James, which was designed by George Fowler Jones, in January 1866. It opened for worship in May 1867 with a service presided over by the Archbishop of York. The first minister was Rev G M Straffen. As in most churches at this time, half the seats were to be free and half were paid for at a yearly cost of fifteen shillings, so the wealthy families had their own pews. Between 1885 and 1904, various additions were made to the building, including a vestry hall in 1902.

The cost of installing the Peal of Six Bells was met by John Roper of Clifton Croft. The eight bell ringers even had a teacher from Oxford to instruct them. After Roper's death in 1875, his partner James Melrose erected the first memorial window in the church, in memory of his good friend. There is also a plate in his memory, and a sum of £500 was invested, the interest to be spent on bread and coal for the local 'deserving poor'.

The second minister was H G Hopkins, and during his time the vicarage and the church school were built. (The rambling 19 room vicarage was actually divided into two in 1954). The church choir started its own cricket club. In 1888 there were midweek services for different members of society, such as a service for young people, a service for 'servants and working-women' and an address for 'professional and business men'. The church also held many social events such as rambles, concerts, magic lantern or limelight lantern exhibitions, games, suppers, ambulance classes, and parties for the Mother's Union. At the Jubilee of Queen Victoria in 1887, the church was decorated with plants and flags were flown from the tower. A memorial cross following the First World War was erected in 1918.

Joan Aherne lived at Clifton Green and her family attended the church.

Grandfather, George Horner, was a bell-ringer. He'd take me to the Minster on Sunday morning quite earlyish, and they would finish there and then come to Clifton.

He was one of the ringers for the first recording of the peal on disc by HMV in 1928.

My mother was born on 24th May, Empire Day, and she used to say 'They rang the Minster bells when I was born'. That was Queen Victoria's birthday as well. I think I did have a pull once or twice. My grandmother was Louisa, there was a little memorial to her in the church. She was a keen member of the Mother's Union, made the teas at meetings. My mother and father were married there, I was christened there and married there.

Horner family. Back L to R – Frank and Ivy Horner, Louisa and George Horner, (Joan's grandparents), Ben Ketley. Front – David Horner, Henry Horner, Joan Ketley
(Joan Aherne née Ketley)

In 1987, the church made news as the Rev Sylvia Mutch was the first woman to conduct a wedding in England, ten days after being ordained as a deacon by the Archbishop of York. As the minister was on holiday, Rev Mutch married Heather Irvine, her former Sunday School pupil, and Alistair Darnley. Their small wedding with 32 guests got taken over by 20 reporters, 15 press photographers and three TV crews! A few years later Sylvia baptised their baby son. She became Rector of Elvington, Sutton on Derwent and East Cottingwith and eventually a priest and honorary canon of York Minster in 1998. Writing about her in the Daily Mail, Anne Diamond said that, 'Sylvia has devoted her life to the church even though she believed women would never be ordained within her career. It's wonderful that she was able to achieve her dream'.

In more recent times, the church was refurbished and the pews removed. But even more radically, the altar was moved from the east side of the church to the west. This meant that the space could be more useful, with several small rooms partitioned off in the main body of the church, and

Clifton Parish Church vicarage (Van Wilson)

coffee tables and chairs for other events. The church is now known as Clifton Parish Church. Next door is the vicarage, the house also includes the church office and a flat.

Lucy Staples 2011 (Van Wilson)

Lucy Staples is a member. She feels that the change has been a good one.

It's been absolutely wonderful not only for the church but rooms are let out for talks and the local Women's Institute have meetings there every month. They took all the pews out, which in some ways is a shame but, on the other hand, the chairs are a lot more comfortable to sit on. There were no facilities for having coffee. They've got a good kitchen there now. They have quite a few concerts and something once a year for the Friends of the Hospital. And the nurses' group, we have a talk there once a year and we have tea and it makes a bit of money for funds.

Joan Aherne also recalls the church hall in Water Lane.

They used to have whist drives, and wedding receptions. I had my 21st birthday party there. There was plenty going on. We had little dances as well. It was quite a big hall.

The hall was sold and demolished and replaced by the Clifton Health Centre. Today the church is thriving and has a fulltime minister, two associate ministers, two curates, a youth worker, a parish co-ordinator and an admin assistant. The main church also has two other churches under its auspices, one at Clifton Moor and St Mark's in Manor Lane, which is, as Joan explains,

part of the parish. They run a lot of it separately but financially it's all in together. The vicar is in charge. Then there's a church up at Clifton Moor, from about ten years ago. It's combined the church and the Methodist, and the Methodists looked after it for five years and then the church for five years. But they still have joint services.

CLIFTON METHODIST CHURCH (Known as the Chapel)

The stone laying for the Methodist Chapel next to St Peter's School was in May 1908 and the church opened in November 1909. Joan Aherne and her family moved to live in Pontefract and when they returned to York, after the war they joined the Methodist chapel in Clifton. Joan enjoyed the services there and recalls,

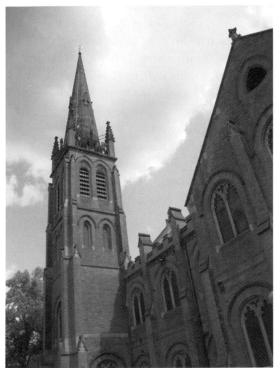

Clifton Methodist Church (Christine Kyriacou)

We were involved in music, the choir at chapel. Both my parents were musical and I play the piano. We enjoyed it. We had the Sunday School anniversary once a year in the summertime, you recited or sang on a platform. We always had a new dress for that. My mother made some things, she was quite a good seamstress. And I used to like a straw hat with little rosebuds on it.

We used to play tennis from chapel in Rawcliffe Lane at the tennis club. And we had a garden party every year either in the Homestead or in Rawcliffe Lane on the left, it's a nursery now. There was a lovely house and we had a garden fête there.

Lena Mills was born in 1920 and has been going to the Chapel

since 1927. In the summer after the service on a Sunday night, we'd go onto the Green for hymn singing. It was amazing the number of people who fitted in. I used to look forward to singing. Mr Calvert, our minister, said, "Lena can we sing Cwm Rhonda?" On Remembrance Day the two choirs of Clifton church and our church did a service where we sang an anthem, one year at Clifton Church and one year at the Methodist.

I was a [Sunday School] *teacher for 41 years. We got about 200 on the premises on a Sunday afternoon. I took the little ones, then the junior. I used to train them up for concerts for the anniversary. It was hard work but they enjoyed it.*

I got a lot of pleasure there. There was only one night when they got obstreperous. I said, "Right you can go home, think about it and decide whether you'll do this concert or not. I'm not doing anymore tonight". So the next week I fully expected there to be no children there but they all turned up and they said, "We're very sorry Miss Mills". I'd give them a certain amount of rope and then I'd say, "That's enough", and they'd settle and I'd no more trouble with them. There were some clever kids amongst them.

They used to have a bazaar every year. And the Sunday School outing at Filey. We took a salad tea, and cakes. Parents would come, and when you've got two buses, it's a lot. We got fish and chips from one of the shops there. They appreciated it. Arthur Saunders was the Sunday School superintendent. Unfortunately he was killed in an accident on the road. He was a very genuine man.

We had the chapel youth club, and then the Guides and Scouts. [They would also go cycling]. We weren't a serious cycling club, we cycled for pleasure. We used to go off on our own every fortnight, met on the coast.

Lena Mills *(The Press)*

In 1987 the Chapel was closed for refurbishment, reopening in early December. Margaret Arnold attends.

It used to be in Avenue Terrace to begin with and then as they got bigger they moved.

When we first used to go, I think we had 150 members and it's gone down. They stopped having a Sunday school because there's nobody there. We now have a man with a little boy and a lady with two children sometimes, that's all.

We sold off the lecture hall [to St Peter's School]. *Then they turned the altar round and refurbished it. He was a marvellous architect. He kept the atmosphere. On our celebration of 100 years we did all sorts of things, had a garden party. It was really good.*

This was held in late 2009 and the Lord Mayor and Civic Party attended the centenary celebrations. Today children's activities centre on Brownies, Rainbows, Guides, Beavers, Cub Scouts, Scouts and Rangers. But in November 2010 teachers from Clifton Green School took a class of 50 children into the church one day aged six and seven to learn about baptism and the minister conducted a 'pretend christening'.

ST LUKE'S

In Victorian times, the Burton Stone Lane area was served by a 'tin tabernacle' in Shipton Street. Then, in 1900, George Faber MP laid the foundation stone for a new church building on the corner of Burton Stone Lane and Shipton Street, to the design of renowned York architect Walter Brierley.

Ten years later, the Archbishop of York laid a second stone to mark the start of work on the nave, which opened for worship in 1911 with temporary brick side walls where two additional aisles were to be added. The church became a parish in its own right in 1927.

St Luke's Church, Burton Stone Lane (Van Wilson)

The church website describes it as 'a strange-looking building from outside, but bright and uplifting inside. Light floods through the huge rectangular clear glass windows of the nave, so that worshipping in St Luke's connects you to the airy beauty of the completed chancel, and to God's world directly outside. Our worship is enhanced and supported by a variety of music, much of which is led by the pipe organ which St Luke's acquired from a closed Methodist Chapel on Teesside in 1959'.

Wedding of Eileen Race and RAF pilot Jack Wood at St Luke's 1955 (Eileen Race)

The church seems to integrate well with the Burton Stone Lane community. In 2010 it held an alternative to Halloween celebrations, The Bright Light Adventure, when a group of local children met to take part in crafts based around the theme of light, making Chinese lanterns, firework pictures, shadow puppets, as well as apple bobbing and making biscuits. There was also an opportunity for children to follow a light labyrinth through the church, with the wise men following a light to find Jesus.

Pauline Wright, who also does the flower arranging, gets involved when

> *each year we put on an activity week and we get about 100 children.*
> *We do a lot of craft things, and Bible stories in a light hearted way,*
> *singing and jokes, they have a fun week.*

The church also has connections with international affairs, and in January 2010 the vicar, Steve Benford, travelled to Haiti following the earthquake, as part of a volunteer surgical team, working as an anaesthetist as he does for two days each week in Northallerton. He is a non-stipendiary minister (unpaid for his work at the church).

Another offshoot of St Luke's is the Sunnydene Players. This group came out of a number of amateur singers, dancers and actors gathering in 1988 to put on an evening of Edwardian entertainment. 'Performing, playing, set-building, costume-making and, of course, watching and encouraging are all valued and seem to engulf a lot of people in and around St Luke's'. The group has also performed as part of the York Wagon Plays since 1994. The church choir is affiliated to the Royal School of Church Music, and choir members work through the award scheme including the Dean's Award.

Another interesting local tie is with the York City Football club. The church organises community carol singing at the Pitchside bar on Grosvenor Road.

On 1st April 2011, the following article appeared on the church website.

'ST LUKE'S SHAMED FOR POOR TASTE, AS PARLOUR PLAN COLLAPSES'

St Luke's Faculty Petition for a 'Five Marks of Mission Tattoo Parlour' on Burton Stone Lane has been rejected by one vote in the York Diocesan Advisory Committee for the Care of Churches.

The finely-balanced debate was lost following an impassioned one-hour speech by Nathaniel Boddy-Pearce, the DAC's expert on the work of York architect Walter Brierley, of which St Luke's is a prime example. He said, 'Brierley conceived these walls as a statement of the unadorned purity of God's creation. To attach to this church a tattoo parlour, would be an outrage not merely against the memory of Walter Brierley, but against simple good taste'.

A photograph of Nathaniel Boddy-Pearce whose face is covered with tattoos completed the article. For a short time, there was great consternation until readers realised that the date at the top of the article had some bearing on it!!

NEW LENDAL CONGREGATIONAL CHURCH

Opposite St Luke's Church, the New Lendal Congregational Church, which seated 300, opened in 1935 to cater for the non-conformists who had attended Lendal Chapel in town, until its closure in 1929. But falling numbers at the Burton Stone Lane chapel meant that in 1994 the congregation joined with St Columba's United Reform Church in Priory Street and the chapel was demolished soon after.

ST JOSEPH'S RC CHURCH

When families from Hungate and Walmgate were rehoused in new council houses in the 1930s, these included many descendants from the Irish families who had come over during the potato famine. Mostly Catholic, the families needed their own churches on the new estates. These included Bell Farm, Tang Hall and Clifton. St Joseph's Church in Burdyke Avenue was built just beyond the intersection of Kingsway and

St Joseph's RC Church, Kingsway (Van Wilson)

Burdyke Avenue in the 1930s specifically for the surrounding estates. It is described as a functional church with no specific architectural features, apart from the tall tower and the statue over the door, of St Joseph the worker. The current priest, Father Ross Thompson, is a married man who moved over from the Anglican church.

On June 8th, 1945, just after the Second World War had ended, the top of the church was hit by a Halifax aircraft, flying back to the aerodrome at Clifton, which resulted in a crash landing next to the nearby Imperial public house. Malcolm Maher was a child and witnessed this event.

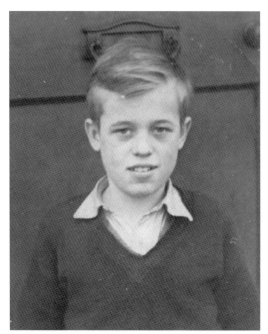

Malcolm Maher as a boy (Malcolm Maher)

Me and Cliff Binnington, he was my mate at school and he lived up Peterhill, was coming down Burdyke and we saw this aeroplane, a right loud noise, you could just see a bit of it. Then we heard a bang, so we ran down Burdyke up to where the Imperial was and this plane was stuck in the actual yard of the Imperial. It had hit one of the wings on the cross [on top of the church] *and turned and crashed. The Imperial yard was fairly big, and it had caught the first house there. There's a big dome and the cross was in the dome and it was on the floor in front of the church. We ran over and someone said they* [the crew] *were still alive, and as young kids we daren't go too near. But they said a few days later that they'd died when they got them out. If you look at the house there,* [next door to what was the Imperial] *you can see the brickwork, it's a different colour from the rest.*

115

St Joseph's Church has a plaque to the RAF crew, pilot Flt Lt Ian Cruikshanks, and engineer Flt Sgt Victor Clare, which was unveiled in 1996 by the pilot's son Air Commodore Colin Cruickshanks.

– Chapter 8 –
DOCTORS AND HOSPITALS

Since the late 19th century, Clifton has been an enclave for the medical profession. As well as surgeries being based there, physicians and surgeons have also made their homes in the suburb. One of the earliest recorded doctors in Clifton was William Belcombe, who died in 1828 aged 71, and has an epitaph in St Michael le Belfrey Church. He founded a private asylum near Clifton Green and was known for his 'humane care'. Dr Belcombe had four daughters and one son, Henry Stephen Belcombe, who continued his father's work and also became a visiting physician to the Retreat hospital. He was a close friend of Dickens who came often to York at this time, partly because his sister in law's family still lived here. Ellen Nussey, the best friend of Charlotte Bronte, put her brother George into the care of Dr Belcombe's Asylum from 1845 to 1853. There is now a street named after the doctors, Belcombe Way off Water Lane, the site of Rawcliffe surgery. On the 1851 census, the matron Mary Ann King was living at Belcombe's Asylum. The inmates were aged from 30 to 77, and were only given initials. Their previous jobs included retired cotton merchant, druggist, retired clergyman, several servants and land proprietors.

In the 1920s a number of doctors resided in the area. Dr Henry Norman Goode was a physician and surgeon at Number 2 Clifton, (he had been appointed Deputy Medical Officer of Health in 1905) and next door at number 1 was James McBride, the medical inspector for the London and North Eastern Railway. At the top of Burton Stone Lane was Dr Montgomery Du Bois Ferguson. Born in Dublin, he came to York to join the medical staff of Rowntree's. He became a GP then assistant physician at the County Hospital in Monkgate. He was in the Royal Army Medical Corps during the First World War, was mentioned in dispatches and awarded the OBE. He became senior physician at the hospital and was sorely missed when he retired in 1939. He moved to Dorset where he died in 1960.

In nearby Bootham were Arthur Lister, physician and surgeon, at number 39, the surgeon Peter Macdonald at 59, George Micklethwaite, another surgeon, at 48, and the Medical Officer of Health, Peter Russell McNaught, at number 50. Cousins John and Wilfrid Gostling (who had a practice in Stonegate) lived at 54 Bootham, which had previously been the surgery of Dr George Augustus Auden, father of the poet W H Auden who was born there. Dr David Rose Cameron was at number 60, and the surgeon Henry Phillips was based just off Bootham, at number 5 Bootham Terrace. Lucy Staples is a retired nurse who recalls,

> *We used to call it Consultants' Row. They were all biggish houses. Possibly they had a room for private patients.*

William Dowell remembers the local doctors,

> *The motor car was something to stop and stare at around 1900. Dr Foster startled his fellow doctors by using his automobile on his rounds. His seniors commented, "How can a doctor arrive at the bedside of a patient all dusty and trembling after riding in one of those contraptions?"*

> *Tarmacadam had not arrived at this period, at any rate not in Bootham or Clifton and it was very muddy or very dusty. I can well recall straw or peat moss spread across the road in Bootham where there was serious illness.*

> *Our family doctors were Dr Evelyn and later Dr Micklethwaite. These gentlemen preferred to visit their patients in a more stately manner, by carriage and pair or single high stepping hackney, with liveried coachman, the doctor in top hat and frock coat, not forgetting the black bag.*

By the 1950s Doctors Cameron, Cobb, Conyers, Follows, Gantley, Oliver, Vergette and Willson-Pepper were all in Clifton. Dr Arthur Bowman Follows who had a surgery at 32 Clifton, (originally St Peter's Terrace) at the top of Burton Stone Lane, retired aged 72 in 1976, having been in practice for 31 years. Today the practice at 32 Clifton is the only one on Clifton itself, with six doctors – Kemp, Ruston, Coe, Field, Field and Shooter, who took over from Drs Bill Gantley and Maurice Oliver. There are two surgeries in Water Lane, the Priory Medical Group practice with four doctors, three of whom are women, and Clifton Health Centre which has four doctors.

The Ball-Dodds were a well-known family of medical practitioners in Clifton. They lived at Clifton Croft. Dr Edward Ball-Dodd was initially in partnership with Dr Royle. He was a keen member of Clifton tennis club, and died aged 62 in 1950. His wife Henrietta was the first female GP in the city. She and her husband were based at 35 Bootham in the 1920s, and had their joint practice at 77 Low Petergate. Henrietta was a doctor for nearly 60 years (1920 to 1979), and died in 1986 aged 95. She was well-liked in the city, and seen as quite eccentric. She was particularly known for parking her small car anywhere in the centre of town. The police seemed to turn a blind eye to this, but sometimes had to go into her surgery in Petergate to ask her to move it.

Their daughter Dr Kay Ball-Dodd also practised in York until her death aged 59 in 1991. Kay's sister Mary Romilly (née Ball-Dodd) had a daughter, Crystal Sophia Romilly, who is a consultant psychiatrist in the south of England.

Jack Willson-Pepper was born in 1904 in Folkestone. After the Second World War he lived at 48 Bootham, later moving to 8 Clifton, becoming renowned as a urology consultant at York County Hospital and York City Hospital. He wrote many articles for the British Medical Society and was a member of the British Association of Urological Surgeons, (specialising in kidneys and urinary tracts). He died in 2000 at the age of 95.

Dr Peter Dench had his practice at the top of Rawcliffe Lane from 1960. As a boy, he helped out at his father's (Dr Reginald Dench), practice in Heworth Green, before going to Cambridge University and training at Bart's (St Bartholomew's Hospital in West Smithfield, London). He started working as a doctor in

the summer of '52, from the time coming out of the army. I was 26. Heworth Green was the main surgery at that time. The three practice surgeries were Micklegate, Heworth Green and Boroughbridge Road. It was pretty large and well-organised. There were still a lot of single handed practices at that time. And this was a new venture. The practice was one of the biggest in the north of England. We had a collector [of doctors' fees] *in Fairway, Mr Clayton. When he retired, we bought his house in Fairway. He collected the dues.* [In the 1930s, a doctor's visit usually cost 3s 6d, and a bottle of medicine took it to seven shillings. Consultation in the surgery was three shillings]. *The National Health Service came in about the time I did. In the*

beginning it was all sweetness and light, there was nowhere you couldn't go with the thing. Many archaic things were swept away. I remember that my mother used to do the dispensing, making up bottles of medicine down in the cellar in Heworth Green. That all became a thing of the past.

When Peter Dench (whose sister is the actress Dame Judi Dench) and his wife Daphne bought the house at Rawcliffe Lane, and opened the practice there, it had to be altered and extended within a few months. They soon had a large number of patients.

Dr Peter Dench (York Oral History Society)

A lot of people from the centre of the city had moved out and Kingsway and Spalding Avenue were part of the move so that a lot of the practice had come out to Clifton.

I went out as far as Skelton [to see patients], *but most of it was within a radius of three quarters of a mile. St Peter's School was looked after by* [Dr] *Edward Vergette who lived in Clifton* [next to the church]. *But quite a number of the staff were our patients.*

We had our days on duty and our nights on, and weekends. Much of the visiting was in patients' homes. In Clifton, many were the hospital lot. They started in general practice, then at the beginning of the National Health Service, they had to opt on which way they were going. [General practice or consultancy]. *We knew everybody. We'd go to the Medical Society in Stonegate, on a Saturday night. I was for a few years on the local medical committee. I can't remember walking into town. I think at that time, we took the car, and we left it in the middle of Stonegate. We had quite a good smattering of consultants at the hospital around. Peter Macdonald lived opposite, he was the eye man before John Magnus.*

Mrs Daphne Dench played a large part in the running of the surgery, experiencing the downside of living in the same house as the practice.

We used to have Saturday surgeries and evening surgeries. It would be full two hours before the surgery, they'd be queuing in the garden. The night [Dr Reginald Dench] *died, we had a waiting room full. They wouldn't go home. I had to go and find another doctor.*

It was so busy, I've often taken him a cup of coffee when he didn't have time to go for lunch. He had an evening surgery and an afternoon one. If he was on a night call, he went out in the middle of the night, and if another call came, I couldn't let him know. He'd go to a phone box and ring me when he'd finished. I had to sit up and wait till he rang me, to say he'd got to go on another call.

Peter explains,

It was very much a two-person thing. It made much more order in life when we got an appointments system. It was a team effort, no doubt about it. If that had gone wrong, one would have been in trouble. We normally went over to Heworth Green in the morning and divided the list, working out who was going to go where. You started about nine o'clock and you were visiting till one o'clock normally. But during an epidemic...one lived in dread of a flu epidemic, because you knew that your life wouldn't be your own. Polio was always a big worry. Not one I came across very often. The Fever Hospital on Huntington Road used to take the serious infected diseases, but we didn't use it very much in my time.

Sometimes patients had to be committed to Clifton Hospital.

There was a chap called the Relieving Officer who was a mental nurse. You had to get him involved and it was horrid really.

Sometimes flooding affected the visiting.

My father used to have the most awful trouble. There was one time, I was in Cambridge, he'd had to do part of his visiting by boat. That was when the Tang Hall beck came up. Water Lane end was flooded one year, about 1980, the kids put crates across for you to walk across. As far as the practice was concerned, the Bridge made more difference than anything really.

Holidays were all right. It was more or less fixed at six weeks. Two weeks used to be Territorial Army, camping, but the other four, you could call your life your own. [Although Dr Dench was once asked for a prescription on the beach in Scarborough!]

They built the health centre [in Water Lane] *about '70, at the end of Kingsway and they said, "There are premises here if you want them". And I tended to resist it for a year or so.*

But eventually Dr Dench did move his practice into the health centre, with nurses, health visitors and other practitioners.

We had a health visitor working with us, Florrie Platts, and a delightful district nurse and midwife. She lived further up Rawcliffe Lane.

I retired just before my 65th birthday, the end of 1989. I'd left York in 1980, I went out to join Robert Porter who was an erstwhile partner. He had set up in Green Hammerton and I joined him for the last ten years. I think it saved my life actually, it was an entirely different way of life. The stress factor went down just like that.

We probably didn't have the amount of paperwork then, as far as I can see. Bureaucracy has grown.

I remember in the five years before I retired, Robert said, "We've got to go onto computers. There's no doubt about it. It's the way things are going". I said, "You can move the computer in the front door when I go out the back". And he did. And it immediately took off and of course it became absolutely invaluable. That's one of the major things that's happened to general practice.

Jack Ruddock was a well-known chemist in Clifton. In the years before the National Health Service, many people would consult a chemist first before paying to see a doctor. He had begun his pharmacy apprenticeship with Oliver Colbert in Fishergate, and qualified at Leeds School of Medicine, opening his own shop in Clifton in 1938. He was appointed vice chair of the Family Practice Committee of the North Yorkshire Health Authority in 1973, and vice chair of the York Health Executive Council. He retired in 1978 from his business at 72 Clifton and died aged 89 in 2002. The chemist's business was taken over by F Wood and Sons after his retirement, a firm from Heworth run by Frederick William Wood and his son Jack Milnes Wood. By 1980 they had nine shops in York and elsewhere. In 1960 they had acquired the pharmacy in Fishergate where Jack Ruddock trained. Jack Wood was Lord Mayor of York in 1973. The rugby ground at Clifton Park on Shipton Road, has a stand named the Jack Wood Memorial Stand, which opened in December 1980.

Jack Ruddock is still remembered with great affection by many Clifton people and is even described as 'an institution'. Gerald Barker knew him,

A service to celebrate the life of

Jack Ruddock

30 August 1912
to
17 June 2002

St Michael le Belfrey Church, York - Tuesday 2 July 2002

Jack Ruddock (Anthony Skeels)

all his life, a super chap, really great guy. I would come into Clifton as a boy when Jack Ruddock's shop had just opened. That was in the days when chemists had their bottles of coloured water in the lovely shaped glasses above the chemist's shop. He really acted as a go-between and the first stage if you had something. The bottle always said 'the mixture', and he would make up concoctions. I remember having something from him which brought me out in a dickens of a sweat, I suppose I had to sweat it out. Ruddocks lived at the back of their shop then he moved to Rawcliffe Lane. Part of that was due to the pressures that used to be put on Jack for people coming for things. They would bother him maybe Saturday night or Sunday and want something completely unnecessary. Although he was such a tolerant and lovely man, he got fed up and bought his house in Rawcliffe Lane.

Peter Dench found Jack Ruddock very helpful.

Jack was my saviour. I mean there were times inevitably when you couldn't read your own writing. It was always good knowing he was there. And there's always that thing, you don't know about having made a mistake, and you knew that Jack would pick it up, and say, "You've put the wrong dosage". Oxygen, you had to find somebody who stocked it. Jack did and so did the people in Intake Avenue. By and large, between the two of them, they looked after that.

CLIFTON HOSPITAL

In 1777, the York Lunatic Asylum opened in Bootham with 30 patients, becoming eventually Bootham Park Hospital. The 'Lunatics Act' of 1845 meant that state provision of asylums became compulsory. The North and East Ridings Pauper Lunatic Asylum on Shipton Road, (designed by Scott and Moffat) on a site of 40 acres, opened in 1847, having taken three years to build. It was situated close to the river at Clifton Ings, because of the clean air outside the city. The original staff consisted of the superintendent, Samuel Hill, his wife Mrs Hill the matron, five male and five female ward attendants, (there was strict segregation), a clerk and steward, porter, cook-housekeeper and several maids, and nearly 150 patients. In the early years, the patients were mostly poor, with about 12 private patients in 1869 which had increased to 56 by 1926.

The buildings were set in large grounds. The male patients worked on the land and female patients helped out in the kitchens and laundry. There was always an emphasis on work as therapy. Two new wings were added in that year, with room for 140, but the demand for places meant that the site had to be extended again in 1856 and 1879. Cottages for staff were also built in the Shipton Road area.

In 1865 some patients were transferred to Beverley and the name changed to the North Riding Asylum which it remained until 1920. This was a difficult time for the hospital. Miss Webb, the assistant matron, died of a fever, and Mrs Hill the matron developed 'a palsy through close associations with the insane' leading to her death in 1866. Within months, Samuel Hill retired with 'entire loss of mental and bodily health'. Dr Thomas Christie replaced him but only stayed for five years. He introduced billiards, cards, newspapers and bagatelle for patients. A school was opened with a patient (ex teacher) in charge, as well as a hospital orchestra.

Joseph Tregelles Hingston came in 1870, having earlier been assistant to Samuel Hill. The asylum had a committee of 21 visitors to oversee its work and make a report. Patients were given more freedom, with trips on the river, to the Gala and the pantomime. Both typhoid and smallpox affected patients so in 1872 there were smallpox vaccinations. The chapel became a recreation hall and a new church was built by the architects Gould and Fisher costing £2,700. The average wage for 'attendants on the insane' was 15 shillings a week plus board and lodging. Rawcliffe Landing was built in the late 1870s, with access through the land belonging to the Earl of Harewood. A dining block and new wards were added and a water tower was erected in 1882. The Asylum fire brigade was formed at this time.

In 1884 the hospital purchased Rawcliffe Farm. From the earliest time, the hospital became self-sufficient and self-contained, with food grown and produced on the farm and in the gardens. The farm had a Guernsey herd to produce its tuberculin tested milk. Coal and other items arrived by barge at Rawcliffe landing.

In 1890-91 an isolation wing was added to the hospital. By 1906 there were 726 patients. Dr Hingston retired in 1905, after 35 years as superintendent, and was replaced by Albert Irwin Eades. Extra padded rooms were installed for suicidal patients around this time and more cottages built for married attendants.

In July 1897 Clifton Parish Church held a 'Grand Bicycle Gymkhana' in the grounds of the hospital, with 'tortoise, cigar, needle threading and potato races' followed by a grand parade of decorated bicycles.

During the First World War, part of the hospital was requisitioned for wounded troops. A nurses' home was built in 1915. In 1920, the name was changed to the North Riding Mental Hospital, which it remained until it became part of the National Health Service in 1948 and was then called Clifton Hospital. The work took its toll on the staff, and Eades, the fourth superintendent, committed suicide in 1924. He was replaced by Dr Ivison Russell. Despite the shock to the hospital, life became more relaxed for patients, and some wards became more 'open'. There were football and cricket pitches as well as a bowling green, library, and film shows, art therapy and entertainment provided by the Rowntree Hospital Service committee. Occupational therapy was an important part of life for the patients.

New treatments were coming in, and it was found that the treatment for malaria could be effective for general paralysis. The Mental Treatment Act of 1930, allowed patients to come in as volunteers. By this decade, 89% of the patients were usefully employed. Shock therapy, which still continues today in some parts of the country, was introduced in 1936.

During the Second World War, part of the hospital was again requisitioned and about 5000 military psychiatric patients came into the hospital during the war years. Volunteers were brought in to run amenities such as the canteen and tuck shop. During the 1942 Baedeker raid, the chapel was badly damaged.

March 1947 saw major flooding at the hospital, and residents in the cottages near the cricket field had to be rescued by boat. In 1953, Greystones, home of the clerk and steward, became an out patient clinic. In 1955, the property called Moorlands, Skelton, was bought to provide relief for the over-crowded hospital. In 1954, the hospital was appointed the centre for leucotomy (later lobotomy) operations and in the 1960s the hospital became a treatment centre for heroin and cocaine addiction. In 1967, Southfields, the former superintendent's house in the grounds, was converted to an adolescent psychiatric unit.

William Fraser was superintendent from 1951 to '65, followed by Dr P J Quinn, who stayed until retirement in 1979. Big changes were made in the '70s and '80s as new ways of treating the mentally ill were adopted. With the advent of more anti-psychotic drugs, admissions reduced.

Sheila Goater lived in Clifton and recalls,

Some of the patients were allowed out. Sometimes they used to laugh and giggle at people and we were told to keep away if we saw anybody 'funny'. There was a place up Shipton Road, a landing stage, where they brought coal and stuff up for the hospital. And it was always referred to as the 'maddies' landing'.

There was quite a lot of involvement with the hospital by Clifton people. Sports events and summer fairs were open to the public, and CHAOS, the Clifton Hospital Amateur Operatic Society, presented shows. Gill May lived on Alwyne Drive and remembers going to the hospital because

As a child I used to sing in the choir on a Sunday morning. There were people in the street who worked there. They must have had connections. As you went up Shipton Road past Alwyne Drive, there were more cottages on the left and people who worked at the hospital.

When we'd walk through the grounds, there was a unit where it was very highly secure, they were all locked up. They'd shout at you through the window. Sometimes odd ones got out, a siren would go letting everyone know that somebody had got out.

Joan Aherne, a member of Clifton Methodist Church, would go to the hospital occasionally.

There was a Gilbert and Sullivan Society at Clifton Hospital, I belonged to that. I made lots of friends there. They used to have, one night a week, a friendly hour, and people from various churches would take part. Patients would come in and I'd play the piano. I think a lot came because they got a cigarette and a nice cup of coffee and they got out of the ward a bit. You'd ask them for their favourites. 'Onward Christian soldiers' and 'Fight the good fight', always the same ones every week. I think they got a lot out of it. It was quite forbidding though, you had to get someone to let you out with a key and lock it behind you. You felt a bit hemmed in.

Roy Hodgson lived near the hospital.

I knew quite a lot of people that worked there. It was self sufficient, they had orchards. We'd go to functions there quite often. They had dances. It was a lovely place, it had a sprung floor, [a Canadian maple dance floor]. *They opened it to the public. It was for the staff mainly but some of the patients were able to go.*

Some of the ladies were in a secure area I think and sometimes they'd get out. There was a cornfield between the hospital and our house and they'd run through the cornfield taking all their clothes off, with the warders chasing after them.

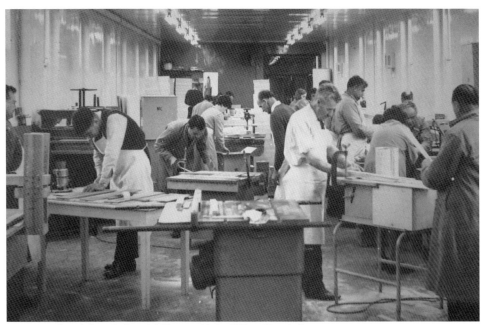

Joiners' workshop, Industrial Therapy Unit, Clifton Hospital, 1967 (Borthwick Institute for Archives)

Clifton Hospital before demolition (Mike Race)

It's a shame it was split up. It was a nice community. There's the Dormouse there now. A lot of offices were built and taken over by Norwich Union. They've now moved to Monks Cross. There's a lot of land. They bought the whole of the land did Persimmon but have only built on part of it. The church is right at the end [and is used for offices].

A nursing cadet scheme was introduced at Clifton Hospital in 1952. Margaret Chapman (née Harding) remembers her time as a cadet nurse there.

They ran a cadet nursing course for 16 and 17 year olds. I was there in 1967 and I left in September 1968. Then I trained at the Retreat. There were about eight cadet nurses. It was quite a busy hospital, and thriving. There were maybe half a dozen black West Indian nurses, I think they came from Barbados. That was very unusual in York. [Because of the shortage of nurses, they were specifically recruited from West Indies and West Africa to fill the gaps].

Margaret Harding at Clifton Hospital
(Margaret Chapman née Harding)

The uniform, the dress was blue and the cape was navy blue and the straps were bright red. You had a six week introduction when they went through psychology, the definition of mental illnesses and what you might look for, teaching people to be aware of mood, and knowing that different sorts of behaviour can indicate that somebody's illness was getting worse. You'd be taught how to observe a patient to see what the levels of their mood were or what was indicated by their behaviour. On the ward, you were kind of thrown in at the deep end and you learnt by experience. William Tuke, the Quaker [who

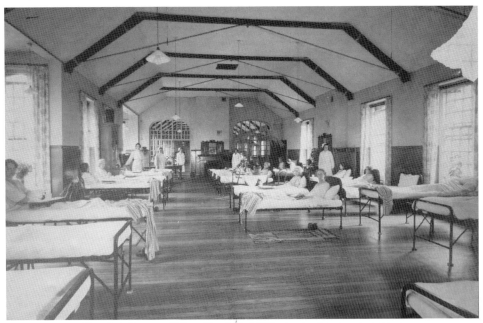

Female infirmary, Clifton Hospital, 1940s (*Borthwick Institute for Archives*)

started the Retreat private hospital in 1796], *was the first person to treat mentally ill people humanely. Before that they were just incarcerated to get them out of the way, there was a huge amount of abuse. Even though he improved things a lot, there was still the stigma. People are much more open to talk about it now. Nowadays they say it's one in five that will have a mental illness in their lives.*

Clifton Hospital had a matron, and a deputy matron who stopped one day to help at the scene of an accident and a lorry came along and knocked her over. So she walked with a very bad limp. And then there were three or four assistant matrons. As a cadet nurse, you spent three months in different departments. It gave you a real understanding of how the hospital worked. Some people went in the supplies department and some in the path lab. I spent three months in the school of nursing, three months in the pharmacy, three months in the stores and three months in the deputy matron's office. I ran errands for her and typed things up. And she would send me up onto the ward to feed the old ladies. There was one ward called the infirmary, and when any of these patients were ill they'd go to the infirmary and be nursed until they died. That was the first time I saw a dead body. Two old ladies on the ward had gangrenous toes. The smell was absolutely horrendous. Then the matron said, "You need to go to the mortuary". They had them in the fridge built into the wall. It really was an introduction into how hospitals work. Working in the pharmacy and knowing how it operated was very useful for when you were on the ward, and you had to order drugs. You knew what the system was. And working in the path lab, you got a good understanding in what the different lab tests were about and how they were operated. The school of nursing was great. Mr Laycock, the superintendent of the school, was really nice. I would type up notes for him, so when the students came in, they'd have all the right things in the right places. I do remember taking the typewriter to pieces, because it wouldn't work, and he got very alarmed, he didn't think I'd be able to put it together but I did. They had a patient who came in and worked there, an old man, he was always in the corner doing something. I think a lot of mentally ill people in those days, it was a stigma, but being in hospital was a safe place to be. If you

*had somebody behaving oddly in the general community, they could
be the victim of teasing, bullying and harassment.*

*The gardens were lovely and the nurses' home was really nice. If you
imagine a long narrow building with a corridor with rooms off each
side and in the middle this area that opened out with televisions and
easy chairs. On the ground floor it was the boys, and the girls were
upstairs.*

Unfortunately, towards the end of its days, there were court cases
involving two senior psychiatrists at the hospital accused of sexual assault.
One was imprisoned and the other was deemed too ill to stand trial, as
he was suffering from dementia. The jury could not agree on most of the
charges and he was only found guilty on one count, though he was put
on the sex offenders register. 38 women made complaints against him
between 1965 and 1988. When the case was taken up by the police, a
total of 67 women came forward, claiming sexual assault or inappropriate
behaviour. One sister at the hospital pursued the matter even when
management dismissed her allegations, and was transferred. No serious
investigation was undertaken until 1997, over 30 years since the first
concern was raised. The Sunday Times set up an investigation which led
to a full inquiry (costing £3.2 million) which came out in 2005, finding
gross negligence by the hospital. The Sunday Times called the whole thing
'a conspiracy of silence...the scandal was not investigated for 20 years
because of excessive respect for and fear of consultants'. The Guardian
in January 2007 stated that 'the 2005 government inquiry found the two
consultants sexually assaulted at least 77 of their patients over a 20 year
period'. Several hundred thousand pounds was paid (by the NHS) in
compensation and there is a survivors' help group.

Clifton hospital had such a good name in its field, especially as a
psychiatric training hospital, but these events now tarnish its reputation.
In the 1980s the policy regarding mentally ill patients changed, and 'care
in the community' was introduced. The hospital closed in 1994 and
most of the site was put up for sale. Part of the site became Clifton Park,

Patients at Clifton Hospital 1889 (Borthwick Institute for Archives)

Crowds wait at Clifton Hospital for the Duke of York, later King George V, when he was awarded the Freedom of the City of York 1893. He visited the hospital and stayed at Fairfield Manor.

a new state-of-the-art NHS treatment centre on Bluebeck Drive, where hip and knee replacements, hernia repair and other joint operations are carried out. The building that originally housed Clifton laundry was converted for use by the Wheelchair Centre in 1996. The former infirmary building for women patients is now Clifton House, a specialist long stay unit providing mental health care. Some of the new streets built on the site used names of wards from the former hospital and Eades Close and Russell Drive were named after two of the superintendents. Rawcliffe Farm has become the Riverside Farm pub and restaurant with a Hungry Horse children's area.

FAIRFIELD SANATORIUM

Fairfield Sanatorium on Shipton Road, a little way from Clifton Hospital, opened in 1920, the first TB sanatorium in the United Kingdom. The building had once been part of Rawcliffe Stud, an important stud farm, and one of the first in the country formed with the specific purpose of making money from breeding racehorses. The company originally had 1350 acres of land, and was owned by Mr H Thompson. In 1850 he set up a company to lease the top four year old, the Flying Dutchman, from Lord Eglinton. One of the stud's great successes was the 1851 St Leger winner Newminster, son of Beeswing. During this time he sired numerous winners, including the famous 1867 Derby winner Hermit. Unfortunately by 1862 the stud was in financial trouble and it was advertised for sale. Thompson set up the Moorlands stud with his son in nearby Skelton and lived at Moorlands House as a gentleman farmer with a butler, cook and three other servants.

During the First World War, a royal field artillery unit was stationed in the grounds of Fairfield. The stables were used as a horse hospital run by the unit's own veterinary surgeons. After the war, there was a need for more sanatorium facilities for discharged soldiers, so the authorities bought the large Georgian mansion (built in 1725 by John Kilby). During the Second World War, the sanatorium gave priority to forces personnel.

Fairfield Manor (now a hotel) (Van Wilson)

Joan Aherne recalls cycling out to visit the hospital,

We'd sometimes go on a Sunday night after chapel to sing. I remember when it was cold, they had all the windows and doors open there and there was nothing to stop the wind. These people were sitting up in bed shivering away.

In 1961 the building became Fairfield Hospital, and patients with chest diseases began to be admitted. Over the coming years, the threat of tuberculosis in England lessened and treatment changed dramatically, until the disease could be mainly controlled by medication. One block of the hospital was converted to a child psychiatric unit in 1963. This closed in 1976 and the unit joined with that at Clifton Hospital to become LimeTrees, the Child and Adolescent Mental Health Service on Shipton Road. The old Fairfield Hospital was sold in 1979 and became the Fairfield Manor Hotel. The Tees East and North Yorkshire Ambulance Service (formed in 2006) is also based on part of the old hospital site. The gardens contain a Victorian ice house which is also a listed building.

TB patients at Fairfield 1963. Bill Wilson seated on left (Van Wilson)

– Chapter 9 –

THE RIVERSIDE

Ouse at Clifton c1900 (Derek Metcalfe)

In the 18th century, the gentry from the city of York would enjoy a promenade by the river to Clifton. They would visit the Marquee and the Maypole, two inns which had tea gardens at the riverside. The Maypole was opened in 1766 by John Dalton of the Punch Bowl in Stonegate. An esplanade was built in the 1840s and a local man, Mr Scruton, sold oranges to promenaders near the White House in Water End in the late 1800s.

Another early attraction was the horse racing which began in 1708 on Clifton Ings. Sir William Robinson who owned much of the land at Clifton and Rawcliffe, offered part of his land for the racecourse. Originally the prize for the winner was a golden ball. But the environment was not ideal and there were problems with flooding so the sport moved to the Knavesmire in 1731.

Originally there was a pond opposite Water Lane, out of which the Burdyke flowed, across the lower part of Clifton Green, and down beside the footpath that leads to Marygate Hamlet. This was the chief means of drainage in Clifton. Water Lane was only a rutted track between farms, the Burdyke running alongside it. When the Water Lane area was built up, one of the streets was named Burdyke Avenue.

FERRY

The River Ouse divided the two suburbs of Clifton and Acomb, with Leeman Road halfway between, but it was not until the mid 20th century that a bridge was built to link the two communities. Before this, a ferry was the means of transport for getting over the river. In the 1902 street directory, John Smith, ferryman, is listed at Clifton Scope Ferry, based at Leeman Road.

Marion Tweedy who lived in Ousecliffe Gardens, remembers the ferry.

My sister in law used to come. When she was first married they lived on Boroughbridge Road, in Lavender Grove. And when she got a baby and wasn't working, she would walk down. Sandy was the ferryman and he'd row her over. If we wanted to go over, we used to call Sandy, and he had like a little railway cabin at the far side. Water End was the road to nowhere, you didn't get any traffic to speak of.

Sheila Goater also recalls,

There were ferries at various places along the riverside. There was one at Clifton Scope which took you across to Leeman Road. You'd go up and shout 'ferry'. I think it was a penny to go across. That was a great pleasure to do that.

The Ferry, Water End (York Oral History Society)

You could walk along the river side right up to Clifton Scope. When I was a child, there was a tree at the corner, where you would come to the bridge now, with a seat all round it. We'd walk [by the river] to school. Where The Avenue is, the stream was still visible, there was a big tree. You could jump over the stream if you climbed up this tree, jumped over onto the other side. Part of the fun of going to school!

Sheila's family lived in Sycamore Terrace.

There were no houses beyond the river end of Longfield Terrace and all that area right to Queen Anne's fields, it was referred to as the Tip. Sometimes there were bricks and things there, [from] when those houses were built, sometime in the 1870s I think, big terraced houses. When we got bikes we'd ride up and down it. But my sister once fell and caught her knee and she had a very deep cut across her knee all her life. She'd cut it on one of these bricks. In Marygate it always flooded in the winter. In 1947 it was the first time it came over the banks and into Longfield and Sycamore.

Pauline Wright enjoyed going to Clifton Ings.

If we were going for the whole day we took a little tent. I remember having picnics. We could go off and play, and your parents, as long as they knew vaguely where you were, didn't bother.

Doug Heald's mother Mabel was very keen on fishing there. He recalls,

We would cycle, bit of fishing, stop at one of the tuck shops and get sweets and a drink. It was wonderful. My mother took fishing very seriously and was a pioneering woman in a man's world. She'd been involved in the hospital cup match which is still fished at Fulford and Bishopthorpe. She wanted to raise money for this orthopaedic hospital. It was called the Renshaw Cup, her maiden name, but the war years changed that and it became the Orthopaedic Hospital Cup Match. All the other mothers relied on my mother to take their lads fishing. She could have up to twelve. She'd have prizes, some little trinket from Woolworth's, and when you're 12 and you're pulling out tommy ruff and gudgeon, you're wanting this prize. The Ings was just another world. The wild openness.

Mabel Heald (Douglas Heald)

Roy Hodgson also remembers,

Somebody came with a big motor torpedo boat and moored it next to where the bridge is now and they lived on that for quite some time. It slowly disintegrated. It was quite a big thing.

Gill May enjoyed the riverside.

As you came out of Alwyne Drive [off Shipton Road] *and crossed over, there was a gravel pathway down. There was like a jetty down there and the sandy bay was next to it. Further along to the right there was a pond and we'd go tadpoling in there.*

There were quite a lot of kids and we went off to play on the Ings and go swimming in the river. We'd cycle up to Overton, put half pennies on the railway line, and wait till a train had gone past and then go and see if it had squashed them. You could hear the trains coming, it would have been steam engines then.

River at Clifton with sugar beet factory (Derek Metcalfe)

FLOODS

Clifton has always suffered with floods. The big floods of October 16th and 17th 1892 resulted from 40 hours of rain. The water mains and railway lines were damaged. A carriage attempting to cross the flooded crossroads at Clifton Green provided great entertainment for the crowd.

The Marygate estate was completely under water. After the severest winter in memory, the 1947 floods were also particularly bad. Council vans went round with loudspeakers warning householders to leave. The RAF took cylinder driers to dry out the houses, and the local pub landlords lent beer crates for people to lift their furniture up. A flood relief fund was started for the most urgent needs. Princess Elizabeth sent a box with fruit and vegetables and tins of dried fruit to each of the householders. She had received the tins as an engagement present from friends in the Commonwealth. After the water went down, the houses were filled with mud and silt. Wallpaper was hanging off, soft chairs and furnishings were completely ruined and metal items rusted.

Roy Hodgson

had flood waters up to our gate in 1947, on Shipton Road. There was about 15 foot of water. They had no valves in the beck, the beck goes across the road, the river came back up the beck and flooded the road

Seagulls on Ouse at Clifton (Mike Race)

for quite a long time. We were fortunate, we could just get out of the house. Clifton Green was under 20 foot of water. There's a main sewer goes down into the river, down behind Westminster Road, it just all came back up.

In the 1968 floods, the newspapers reported that thousands of frogs were washing out of spawning ditches upstream so that there were stories of 'raining frogs' in the Marygate and Clifton district.

CLIFTON BRIDGE

A bridge over the river at Clifton had been mooted for over 50 years. The amount of debate over the bridge seems to have exceeded any other council matter. In October 1913, councillors voted for a bridge but changed their minds a month later. The cost would have been £35,000 then, but when it was finally built, in October 1963, the bill came to £230,000. Preliminary work had got underway in 1955 but was halted

Bailey Bridge 1961 (York Oral History Society)

Opening of Clifton Bridge 1963 (The Press)

until a grant could be guaranteed. The Ministry of Transport hinted that it favoured Fulford for funding.

In 1950, the Yorkshire Gazette reported on the proposal to build a Bailey Bridge at Clifton Scope, but it did not happen. In 1961, when the wedding of the Duke of Kent and Katherine Worsley took place in York Minster, it was essential that a bridge was in place to cope with the extra traffic, and so soldiers built a temporary Bailey Bridge. It was so effective that it was impossible to deny the need for a permanent bridge, and this was agreed. It was built with 4000 tons of concrete and 50 tons of reinforced steel, and opened by Lord Mayor Archibald Kirk on October 28th 1963. By 1970, 10,000 vehicles a day were crossing the bridge.

ROWING CLUBS
The River Ouse is very popular with boat clubs and there are always regattas and races in the summer. The first informal regatta on the river was in 1843, and the first formal one in 1865 which started at Marygate

Barge at Maddies Landing (*Mike Race*)

Sandy bay at Maddies Landing (*Mike Race*)

landing. As well as the York City rowing club, there are boathouses by the river for York University, St John's University, Leeds University and St Peter's School.

The map for the 'Yorkshire Head of the River Race' shows Clifton Bridge, and the stretch of the Ouse leading up to Rawcliffe Landing, with Maddies Landing about halfway between, before the outer ring road bridge. This was originally the stopping place for barges bringing supplies to the hospital farm. There is still a track from the landing up to a gate, which then leads to Riverside Farm, once Clifton Hospital farm.

Roy Hodgson remembers seeing

plans for Clifton Ings where they were going to make a marina, in the '30s, I think. That land is used for grazing cattle. Mr Plummer had the plans, they were going to have a club house just along from where Clifton Bridge is, where it's quite high, behind the Homestead.

For whatever reason it didn't... because of the war I suppose. It would have been nice if they'd done that, it would have been a lovely amenity for the city, to have a boating area.

The marina idea resurfaced in the 1960s, but it did not materialise.

RAWCLIFFE MEADOWS

The boundary of the old Clifton hospital site is adjacent to the 25 acre Rawcliffe Meadows Nature Park on the Clifton flood plain, managed by the Friends of Rawcliffe Meadows and established in 1991. Clifton Ings is situated close to the

York sign at Rawcliffe Landing (Mike Race)

Meadows, being separated by the Ings Dyke.

The Friends spent the first few years clearing the area of weeds and creeping thistle and planting new trees and shrubs and establishing a wildlife pond. They now have 180 different types of grass and wild flowers. The rare tansy beetle, (so called because it feeds on the tansy plant), a protected species, is found there in summer. It also became one of the early Countryside Stewardship sites, where skylarks, linnets, snipe, yellowhammers, lapwings, sand martins, willow warblers, chiff chaffs, and corn buntings can be seen.

Rosanne Bostock lived off Howard Drive, Shipton Road in the 1960s before much of Rawcliffe was built up. She enjoyed the countryside.

I got a bike when I was seven or eight. I used to go on my bike towards Fairfield Manor. There were some bluebell woods which were nice and there was no layby then. They built the layby years later, took a great big chunk of the woods away.

I was interested in nature, and collecting flowers. I just wanted to know what everything was, what the trees were, and what birds there were. When I was four, before I went to school, I used to know what the mushrooms were, in the countryside. I seemed to instinctively have an interest.

I never encountered anybody in the woods, I just liked to go and have a bit of peace and solitude. There were no houses at the back of us so we went out of our back garden and it was just fields. You could go rambling for miles, I remember it all being quiet and peaceful. Now it's so built up, car showrooms and supermarkets, it's sad really.

There was a lot of wild land before they started building. Where the shops are now on Shipton Road, that run across from the Mitre, that was all waste land, with wild roses growing and a really nice old fashioned hedgerow. We had a den in there. It was lovely with all the mayflowers and rambling roses. There was quite a lot of wild life down there, lots of foxes.

In the early 20th century, Rawcliffe township had 89 inhabitants. The landowners were Thomas William Tew, the trustees of Earl de Grey, the North Riding Asylum (Clifton Hospital) and Robert Charles de Grey Vyner who lived at Fairfield Manor, a stud farm. After the Second World War, the development of Rawcliffe began, which continued in earnest in the 1970s and '80s, changing the area dramatically from countryside to large suburb.

Clifton Ings 1912

– Chapter 10 –

SCHOOLS

ST PHILIP AND ST JAMES' NATIONAL SCHOOL

Clifton National School for girls and infants, also known as Burton Stone Lane School, opened in 1841 with a schoolroom and a classroom with accommodation for 66 girls. In 1874 the fees were threepence for girls and twopence for infants. In 1878 the girls were transferred to the new school in Clifton, and Burton Lane continued as an infants' school, which closed in 1892 and was later demolished.

Clifton Church School (*Mike Race*)

The foundation stone for the St Philip and St James' National School for Girls and Infants, next to the church of the same name, was laid by Lady Mayoress Elizabeth Melrose on 25 September 1878. The first headmistress was Miss Bedford. It was built for 125 children at a cost of £1,200 and fees were initially 12s 6d. There were 86 pupils by 1879. In 1891 fees were dropped to one penny per pupil and the school's name was changed to the Clifton Church of England Controlled Primary School. The infants from Burton Lane were moved to the school in 1892. By 1900 attendance was free. In 1914 additional accommodation for infants was obtained in the parish hall in Water Lane. In 1928 the school also admitted boys. Numbers started to dwindle and the school eventually closed in 1961 and is now a private house.

Sheila Goater attended in 1929.

This was a little two roomed school, and the youngest ones were in one room and when you went into the upper infants you were in the other room. I have a vivid memory of the first day, there was a great big fire with a fireguard round it, and the headmistress standing in a bright red dress. I first tasted cocoa there. At playtime we all went into a little kitchen and were given a tin mug.

When I started school I'd been very ill, I'd had double pneumonia just before I was ready to start. My mother was a teacher but married women couldn't teach in those days, but I could read and write when I went to school.

There were a lot of children there, some came from Marygate which was quite a poor area. With us being Catholics, my mother sent me to the Bar Convent after that.

There were several small private schools in Clifton in the late 19th and early 20th century, like those run by the Misses Ankers, and the Misses Mary Anna and Jane Husband, the two sisters of Maria Husband who provided the horse trough on Clifton Green. Their school was at Burton House at the top of Burton Stone Lane. At the top of Queen Anne's Road, a small school was run in the 1840s-50s by Frances Haden, her sister and two other teachers aged 41 and 20, to teach French and English. In 1851 they had 16 girl pupils aged 14 to 17, who came from Berwick, Sheffield, Leeds, Mansfield and even as far afield as Scotland.

EBOR PREPARATORY SCHOOL

Ebor Prep School was originally at 116 Clifton, on the corner of Abbey Street. The school had four classes, from nursery to seniors. The top class

Ebor Preparatory School badge (Van Wilson)

was in the attic of the house which caused some consternation as it was a fire risk.

Margaret Arnold attended when she lived at the Bumper Castle on Wigginton Road.

It was during the war, it was '42, and they let me have a pass and I could cycle through the aerodrome and then come up Water Lane to school. Nobody took any notice, they just waved as you went by.

Mrs Loadman used to take us for singing and dancing and we put a show on in the ballroom of the Clifton Cinema. I stayed there until I was about eight and then I went to York College for Girls.

Pauline Wright lived in Burton Stone Lane.

It was wartime, and when I should have started [at Shipton Street] *I got chicken pox and measles and there was too many in the class, over 60. I supposedly went to Ebor School for a term or two but I stayed there until I was 11. It was small, about 65 pupils. The principal was Miss*

Ebor Preparatory School, 116 Clifton
(Van Wilson)

152

Weymouth. Mrs Loadman came after a year or two and eventually she took over as principal. One of the teachers, her husband was in the army, Mrs Green. I liked her, she was young. Miss Weymouth seemed very old. I suppose anyone over 20 is old to a four year old.

It was a very happy school. They used to take quite a lot of children from RAF Linton families because they'd only be there for 18 months or two years. Where Clifton Green school is now, [in Water Lane] *that was a cricket field and there was a wooden pavilion at one end. We used to play rounders and hockey on there. The other side of the lane, York College for Girls used that for their sports field.*

As the area got built up, Ebor lost its outdoor sports facilities. The church hall in Water Lane was used for dancing, and for fencing classes. The school tended to concentrate on the arts subjects, with little science or geography.

Nora Loadman retired as head of Ebor in 1985 at the age of 89. She had begun teaching at St Margaret's School in York in 1918 after training at Wolverhampton. She moved to teach at Ebor in 1943, becoming headmistress a few years later. Her husband Russell Loadman had moved from his farm in Gate Helmsley to run a garage on the site of what is now the Spar supermarket. Mrs Loadman was succeeded by her deputy Valerie Tildesley but she continued to live at the school, stating in an interview with the Yorkshire Evening Press,

I had to stop teaching after the school inspector said I was getting too old, but I am not really. I have a sitting room at the school where I read a lot, crochet, and have the children come in to talk to me and show me what they have been doing.

Talks were taking place in 1999 about moving the school to Rawcliffe Lane as numbers were increasing. In 2001 the school won the Primary Schools' Chess Championship. The school moved in September 2002 to become Bootham Junior School for 3-11 year olds in Rawcliffe Lane, a much bigger school with its own playing fields.

CLIFTON PREPARATORY

There was always a bit of rivalry between the two prep schools, Ebor and Clifton Prep, known as Miss Meaby's, situated in The Avenue. Both uniforms were brown and gold. The latter was founded in the 1890s. Miss Phyllis Meaby, who lived in Westminster Road, was the well loved headmistress. She retired in 1959 after 26 years as head, was succeeded by Ruth Robinson, but continued to help with administration. She died in 1993 aged 94. In 1994, Clifton Prep became the pre-prep school for St Peter's School, for 3-8 year olds, and in 2001 moved to the St Peter's campus.

The school now has about 175 children from nursery to year three, and works closely with St Olave's and St Peter's, although they have separate buildings and head teachers.

PRIMARY SCHOOLS

The growth in population in Clifton and Clifton Moor has resulted in new primary schools in the last two decades. Burton Green Primary is on Burton Green, the road which links the end of Burton Stone Lane with Kingsway North, Clifton Green Primary is on Kingsway North itself and Lakeside Primary School is situated on Oakdale Road, Clifton Moor.

Sheila Audsley, the head teacher of Clifton Green Primary, retired in 2010 after 37 years in teaching, and was awarded the CBE for services to education. In 2001 she led the merger of Kingsway Junior School with Shipton Street infant school to form Clifton Green Primary School. In 2009 the school was awarded an 'outstanding' judgement by Ofsted. One of its after school clubs, the Clifton Green Dance Club, took part in the York Schools Dance Festival several years in a row.

CLIFTON WITHOUT PRIMARY SCHOOL

Clifton Without Primary School, in Rawcliffe Lane, opened in 1928. Rosanne Bostock attended in the early 1960s.

Clifton Green Primary School dance club 2005. Jessica Willis is number 7 (Jessica Willis)

We lived off Howard Drive, Shipton Road, near where the Mitre pub is. But because they were new houses, it was all fields at the back. You'd walk over the fields, there was a plank over the beck and you had to walk over that to take the short cut.

The school was pretty much as it is now. There was a verandah which ran alongside the classrooms and it was all open on the inside. It started with Year One and you just leapfrogged from classroom to classroom as you got older. There was a big hall at one end and the cloakrooms at the other. You were split into A and B groups, they were all A classes on the verandah side. We used to have PE in the hall and we had sports day on Canon Lee fields.

It was still in the days when you got milk in little bottles. In winter it was frozen and in summer it was curdled. I quite liked the lessons, there was a great emphasis on good arithmetic and spelling. You had a spelling test on a Friday before lunch and you couldn't go for lunch until you'd spelt the words. We listened to the radio once a week and had a nature lesson. We went out down Water Lane to the newt ponds (they call it Clifton Backies now). We had handwriting lessons, we'd use an inkwell and a pen with an old fashioned nib. We did sewing as well. Some people made skirts and some made tops and I made a nightie and lined it all with bias binding. When I'd made it, I had to go and get changed and model it, which was embarrassing.

It was quite a big catchment area. Children from Kingsway North came, and right up to the new houses near the Mitre. There were 38 in a class. In our class there was a girl whose dad was a bank manager and some of the children were quite disadvantaged. There was quite a big gap.

The teachers were horrible to everybody basically. They maybe had their favourites but you couldn't get away with anything. Once a boy

Clifton Without Primary School. Rosanne Lomax, 2nd from right on front row
(Rosanne Bostock (née Lomax))

next to me splattered ink on my satchel and I must have been trying
to rub it off and I got into trouble for not paying attention and had
to stand on the chair and everybody was sniggering. I told my mum
when I got home and she wrote a letter. They were so intimidating,
you couldn't speak up for yourself. There was still corporal
punishment and you'd get whacked with rulers and blackboard
rubbers. I don't think they recognised special needs. There was a boy
in our class, I think he was probably dyslexic and he couldn't really
concentrate and found the lessons difficult. She was always hauling
him up and smacking him on the hand with the ruler. All they cared
about was keeping the class quiet so if you couldn't do the work, you
were pretty lost.

Clifton Without was the junior school for its neighbour, Canon Lee
Secondary School, though not all pupils moved there.

In the last two years, Rawcliffe Infants' School on Eastholme Drive has
amalgamated with Clifton Without to form the 'Clifton with Rawcliffe
Federation'. The Infants' school takes pupils up to year two when they
transfer to Clifton with Rawcliffe Junior School (previously Clifton
Without). Both schools will be in the Eastholme Drive building by
September 2011.

CANON LEE SECONDARY SCHOOL

Canon A R Lee School was important because, when it was founded
in 1941 at a cost of £24,000, it was really to cater for the North Riding,
which included northern York, and the villages of Skelton, Shipton and
Beningbrough. There was space for 320 children. The school was named
after Arthur Robert Lee who was ordained in York in 1909 and served
his curacy in Sheffield. His great claim to fame was shaking hands with
Buffalo Bill Cody as a child in the 1870s. He married Olive Wood, who
was later the godmother of Dame Judi Dench. Lee was on the North
Riding Education Committee for 35 years and Diocesan Education Officer
for ten years, as well as Rural Dean of York, and was involved in the setting
up of several York schools.

When Sir Bedford Dorman, chairman of the North Riding Education Committee, formally opened the school on 9th May 1941, he said that being on the border of the city and in an agricultural district would help to 'bridge town and country'. Some of the pupils travelled up to 15 miles to school. The first head was Mr J Storey, and most of the staff were female because of the war.

There were five acres of playing fields, a library, gymnasium, handicraft and science rooms, a laundry, and rooms for the doctor and dentist. There were initially eight members of staff and 184 children which included 22 evacuees. The only day the school was closed was on 29th April 1942 due to the Blitz on York. A bomb blew off much of the roof of Clifton Without junior, and broke most of the windows of Canon Lee. Local people who were bombed out were sleeping on mattresses in the hall and classrooms. The school was used as the ARP (Air Raid Precautions) headquarters for Clifton and Rawcliffe, and the office was situated in the boiler house underneath the building. During the war the school held gardening lessons when each class had a plot for growing vegetables, herbs and flowers. The pupils went to church on Wednesdays from 8.45 to 10am. At the end of the war the girls were encouraged to knit jerseys for poor children in Europe. In 1948 there was a new intake of teachers as men returned from the war.

The school had two weeks half term holiday in October so pupils could go potato picking. It also began to be used as an Evening Institute several nights a week, offering dancing, keep fit, dressmaking and shorthand. It became Clifton Adult Education Centre in the 1970s.

In 1970 Canon Lee became one of the first 11-16 comprehensive schools in North Yorkshire, and was extended with a new gym, home economics and textiles rooms, laboratories, staff room and offices. The cookery room became an art room.

Gill May attended Clifton Without and then Canon Lee.

Coming from a small school, it was quite big. You probably were a bit overwhelmed by it, loads of people there, all a lot older than you. Buses used to come dropping kids off down Shipton Road, there would be a lot from farming areas. One of the girls, her uncle had a farm at Wigginton. I used to go there sometimes with her.

In the senior school, it was navy blue skirt and cardigan with white blouse and maroon tie. Maroon beret and a blazer, with the school logo on.

Canon Lee School. October 1959, Gill May far left on front row (Gill May)

Sport was quite important, and the hockey and cricket teams were successful. About 50 per cent of the school boxing team also boxed for York. In 1950 a pupil from the school, L Donaldson, won the Yorkshire Schoolboys boxing championship. The school was quite progressive in organising trips for its pupils. There were visits to Helmsley and Rievaulx Abbey, as well as an annual excursion to Carberry Tower near Edinburgh.

*We went to London and we went to Germany one summer with the
school, near Heidelberg. I liked science. That was Mr Cooper. I think
he was quite a young teacher. Probably I enjoyed maths the most and
I was interested in domestic science. I learnt sewing at home because
my mother was a dressmaker. We learnt how to make dresses, follow
the pattern, how to cut it out and that sort of thing. I remember
making bread and I remember Irish stew. You didn't always do
cooking, we learnt how to clean, how to wash floors and hygiene.*

As head girl, I used to do things within school [the office]. *And I had
to get the bus into town and go to the bank. Whether it was because
I wanted to go onto secretarial college, I've got no idea. I remember
we always had assembly on a Friday and we used to sit on the stage.*

Gill's elder brother Peter Dale also attended the school.

Canon Lee School shield 1955 (Peter Dale)

*During the Second World
War, a bomb dropped in the
Clifton Hospital fields near
North Cottages and on the
opposite side of the road from
Alwyne Drive. A piece of
shrapnel entered our house
through the toilet window and
the blast caused some cracking
of the house wall.*

*I believe the school population
did not exceed 200 in this
period and in fact my class,
the A form, had no more than
20 in it, of which there were
only eight or nine boys. The
school was very good at sports
and Mr Telford, I recall, was
very enthusiastic. I made the
school shield whilst in Ron*

Southgate's art and craft class in the latter part of 1955 (when I was head boy). The four Yorkshire roses, one large and three smaller, were all hand carved by me. The last time I looked through the window into the assembly hall the shield was still above the stage.

Burton Stone Lane County Secondary Modern School for Girls opened in October 1942, with the senior girls' department from Shipton Street School forming the nucleus. It closed in 1985 and is now Burton Stone Community Centre. For more information and people's stories about the school, see my book 'The Best Years of Our Lives? Secondary Education in York 1900-1985'.

St Peter's Pre-Prep School *(Christine Kyriacou)*

St Peter's School *(Van Wilson)*

ST OLAVE'S AND ST PETER'S

St Peter's public school claims to be the oldest school in England, and one of the oldest in Europe, dating from AD 627. It was founded by St Paulinus, the first Archbishop of York. The ninth headmaster, from 778 to 782, was the renowned scholar Alcuin. For several centuries, the headmaster was an ordained member of the Church of England. The school moved to Clifton in 1844.

There were 65 boys in 1900. Between 1908 and 1919 various properties close to the school were acquired for additional accommodation, and St Olave's, a small private school, was taken over to be the preparatory school for St Peter's, catering for 8-13 year olds. The school formed a combined cadet force in 1914 which carried on for many years. A swimming pool was built in 1922, new playing-fields were opened in

1924, and a library in 1927. By 1925 there were 85 junior boys and 215 seniors (over 12). More alterations were made in the 1930s.

By the 1970s the school had a boathouse on the river, a miniature rifle range, squash courts and hard tennis courts. In summer pupils were offered cricket, rowing, tennis and athletics. In autumn they played rugby and hockey. The pool was used for swimming and water polo.

St Peter's School 2010 (Van Wilson)

Girls came to the school in the 1990s. They initially joined the sixth form and slept in nearby private homes or a hostel under the supervision of a master and his wife. The school has four boarding houses, Dronfield, (after the headmaster there from 1937 to 1967), and The Rise for girls, and Linton and The Manor for boys and six day houses.

Hugh Murray was a pupil at both schools.

I went to St Olave's School in September 1943, and up to St Peter's until summer 1951. My father moved to Doncaster and I was a boarder in 1946. Alan Wentworth Ping, the headmaster of St Olave's, was a First World War soldier. He'd been wounded and he had some kind of calliper on one leg and a spring to make it work. He generally rode a bicycle round the school. When he was at the science lab where he taught, and his bicycle was at the other end of the school, he'd stand outside the science lab and shout out, "Bring me my bicycle". And whoever was nearest to his bicycle used to take it down to him.

There was bomb damage there. One of the buildings hit was the dining block. There wasn't room for everybody to eat, so junior boys were sent to the British Restaurant in Burton Stone Lane. And they had awful meals there. On one occasion I was talking to an old lady, saying that I used to go to the British Restaurant, and I was about to launch into how awful the food was, and she said, "Oh that's interesting, my sister and I ran it". So I was saved the embarrassment! That was Nonie Rowntree, she and her sister Faith ran the British Restaurant. [See page 53]

When I first went, there were only four houses but after three years they reformed a house called the Grove which had been closed. I moved to the Grove, number 17, on the city side of the school. Beyond it was the headmaster's house, St Catherine's. John Dronfield [the head] *was brought in to turn the school around in about 1937 and the school took on a new life when he came. Robert Harding, my housemaster in my final year, and a rugby blue, would have played for England except he damaged his leg. He was a great housemaster. He ran the house very efficiently and without any problems. He just had a natural knack of dealing with small boys. The masters generally were quite old. A number of young ladies from teacher training colleges came, Miss Allen, Miss Mason, and a French lady. They were only 18 year olds. They seemed very much older than us, but Miss Allen who married John Nicks, was only six years older than me.*

The fagging system was still on the go. Prefects had a personal fag and the monitors had the call of all the juniors. They'd come to the study door and shout, "Fag", and the duty fag would appear and do what was required. I was the fag for a fellow called Vince Gregory who was the drummer in the school band. He had an enormous leather apron on which he hung his big drum. That had to be whitened with Blanco, that was one of my jobs, to whiten his leather apron, amongst other things, running messages, tidying up the study. You did quite a lot of things.

I rowed and played rugby, my two principal sports. I rowed in the school first eight and I played in the school second fifteen at rugby. Down Westminster Road there's a cut through that leads to the river, there's a school boathouse there. We started at Clifton and rowed to Lendal Bridge and sometimes there were shorter races that went to a thing called the diving board, by Scarborough Bridge. We had an

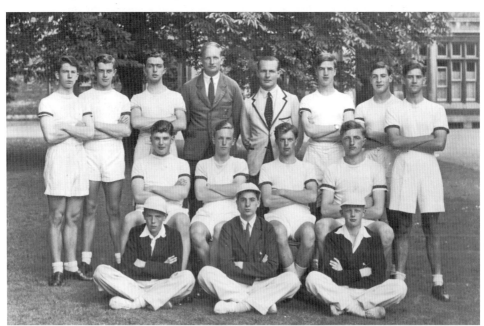

St Peter's boat club 1951. Hugh Murray seated in front of Mr Lavender, the master in white blazer. (Middle row, 2nd from right) (Hugh Murray)

open air swimming bath which had opened in the 1930s. It was filled up with fresh water every now and again. It wasn't heated and, over the summer, algae used to grow so the water got greener and greener until it was too thick to be healthy then it was emptied and new water put in. To try and stop algae growing, we'd put chlorine in. One of my duties was to go down every evening with a jam jar full of chlorine and tip it in the water to try and kill the algae. It never did, we just had this pea soup all the time.

We used to do cross country runs on the Ings. There was an area known as the golf course because, before the war, an old couple used to sit in a little hut and hand out clubs and balls and they had a pitch and putt course. We'd start on the golf course and run right round the Ings and back.

We got a master called Freddy Wayne who took over music and he revolutionised the school music. Not everybody played instruments but he got people involved in choirs and singing, and even coached the school brass band. He had an assistant called Mr Wicks. You may remember the hymn, 'Till moon shall wax and wane no more', we translated that into 'Till moon shall Wicks and Wayne no more'.

I preferred boarding to being a day boy, coming and going. You had to come back to chapel on Sunday evening but when you were a boarder, you were there all the time, so you had your mates around you. I enjoyed it when I got settled in. Leaving home in '46 to become a boarder, it was a great break, but from that time I lived in institutions. School, university and the RAF so I became institutionalised. The people I joined the RAF with were all homesick because they'd never left home before, but I'd had school and university, so I was not fazed about living away from home and away from parental control. I was 24 by the time I went in the RAF so I got a commission. I was an applier of discipline rather than a receiver of it.

When parents came to visit, we had to get an official Exeat and that allowed us out for half a day on a Saturday or a whole day on a Sunday. I remember there were rules, and monitors had to make sure they were observed. Silly rules like 'no hands in pockets' or 'no running in corridors' or 'no whistling'. But they allowed us to practise leadership skills by making sure people did what they were told. I was a house monitor in my last year. Each house had a school prefect who ministered justice and discipline throughout the school. Prefects wore blue gowns to show that they were something special.

When you were a junior you couldn't put your hands in your pockets at all and you couldn't unbutton your jacket. When you became a junior middle, you were allowed one hand in the pocket, and then a senior middle, you were allowed two hands in the pockets, and when you became a senior, you could unbutton your jacket. Silly rules which nowadays people would laugh at. But they allowed people to get the idea that discipline was something that

St Peter's School CCF on its way to Fulford Barracks to be admitted into the East Yorkshire Regiment. Hugh Murray is sailor leading the Naval contingent, just behind the band and the RSM
(Hugh Murray)

166

had to be instilled in you.

The punishments were not lines. We had a card where you had to write out a lot of useless dates. 1815 Battle of Waterloo. 1827 Battle of Navarino. But then it changed to a discipline card, which had a whole pile of guff about discipline. We had to write that out on a foolscap piece of paper. I preferred being caned. It was over and done with, whereas if you had a card to write out, you wasted half an hour or three quarters of an hour on it.

In my time in St Peter's I had 64 strokes of the cane in various fours and sixes, for various activities like being found in the wrong place at the wrong time. I was found exploring the organ loft on one occasion which was strictly out of bounds. I was interested in what happened in the organ loft. It's the only one I can remember specifically why I was beaten. I've been beaten by the housemaster and even the headmaster. Nowadays you'd be up for assault but we accepted it, it was the norm. I'd previously been at school in Wales, in Brecon, where every master had a cane and if you didn't get your answers right, it was one on the hand. Those schoolmasters were all Victorian parsons who were brought out of retirement to teach, when the younger teachers went to fight. They brought Victorian values with them and the cane was part of it.

When Hugh moved back to York in later life, he found a house in Burton Stone Lane.

And as it happened, it was a house that I knew of, because when I was in the Manor House, we'd go out at night to Pratt's fish and chip shop down Burton Stone Lane which was strictly forbidden. We'd go down St Peter's Grove, through a garden, climb over a wall into another garden and out into Burton Stone Lane. And the wall we climbed into was the house that I eventually bought.

We were a quite enclosed community. In the school plays, boys acted the girls' parts, we didn't bring in girls from other schools to do that so we didn't rely on the community for anything, we were self sufficient. But we were seen to be part of the [Clifton] *community. We had to wear caps and if we were seen in the town without caps, somebody would ring up the headmaster. One of the privileges of being a monitor, you didn't have to wear a cap. We wore brown jackets so we were known as Peterites. I went to see a football match at Bootham Crescent and we weren't allowed to go to football matches. I just put my cap in my jacket pocket, I was still wearing my brown jacket. I thought I was escaping observation which in fact I did on that occasion. We were a rugby school and we played with an oblong ball. We couldn't have anything to do with round balls, we weren't even allowed to kick one about in the school grounds. That was a punishable offence.*

When we became monitors we were allowed to go to the theatre. We used to sit in the gods for sixpence looking down at the stage. We were allowed extra privileges, we didn't have to be in bed by ten o'clock.

I remember J X Prendergast offering the school the facilities of Clifton Cinema for speech days because his son John Barry was a contemporary of mine, exactly the same year. He played the bugle in the school band. There were about 250 in the whole of St Peter's.

We didn't think about girls in those days. They came later. Sex wasn't on the agenda. We were a monastic establishment I suppose. We did have one girl we used to admire, Diana Rigg, because her brother was at the school. So when visiting came around and this gorgeous female would come and see Hugh Rigg, we were all full of admiration.

Nowadays grammar schools are old hat and public schools are I suppose. It's elitist I know but you get a better education. St Peter's had a tradition of taking farmers' sons from the East Riding. Some of them didn't want to be educated and left when they were 16 to go and be farmers again. I think about four of us went to university from the whole of the year. Nowadays nearly everybody goes. At that time, it was quite unusual. I was three years in the sixth form and my last year I was doing scholarship level. In fact I went to Oxford and sat the common entrance exam at my college.

Nick Banks went to St Olave's Junior School at the age of eight in 1955.

Wentworth House, St Olave's School 1961. Nick Banks back row 5th from right (Nick Banks)

I spent five years as a day boy. When I went to St Peter's I did become a boarder. In the late '50s, Clifton was very much a village with just local shops and a local community of which St Olave's and St Peter's was quite a big part because of the size of the school and length of time it had been there. Being a boarder meant that the vast majority of your friends went home on a night and you stayed there. You had to get new friends. They came from all over the world. One of my friends lived in the Gambia.

There was about two hours homework every night. I think the discipline and attitude of the school and the way you were developed meant you did think it was the best school. I think you question anything – education, discipline, regime. It was very much its own identity and was quite cut off to some extent. You [were told] *that you must uphold the reputation, must behave yourself, you were representing the school.* [In 1962, Field Marshal] *Montgomery came and told us about discipline and behaviour.*

It was all boys, you had an interest in the opposite sex, and that was frowned on because they hadn't been vetted, they hadn't been approved. We used to enjoy sports days. Girls [from Queen Anne's School] *would come and play on the tennis courts and we'd enjoy the close proximity, but we were not allowed to mix.*

There were one or two girls who lived in Clifton who became friends. I got to know the headmaster's daughter quite well and she lived near school. That was quite interesting, in the holidays going to visit her at the headmaster's house. It's a massive campus. You've got the main frontage and you've got boarding houses up Bootham along with the headmaster's house. Then on the other side you've got one of the boarding houses on the corner of St Peter's Grove and ones in The Avenue. Behind the main framework of the school were playing fields. They stretched down to the river where the boathouse was. The to-ing and fro-ing across the road [in Clifton] *was immense. I think they were concerned with the amount of traffic and safety of the pupils.*

The death of five year old Anthony Mitchell Howat, son of St Olave's headmaster Tudor Howat, in March 1949, started a campaign for a footbridge across the road from the school. It took many years for this to happen. The school even appealed to the Ministry of Transport over the council's refusal to allow a bridge. York City Council finally gave permission and the bridge was built in 1965. It won a Civic Trust design award in 1966. The school rules now insist that pupils must cross the road by the footbridge.

In 1984 a woman cyclist narrowly escaped death when a lorry carrying an excavator demolished the footbridge. The span of the bridge was knocked from its stanchions. The bridge had also been hit ten years earlier in 1974. There have been no accidents since then.

Nick Banks was in

Manor House, in St Peter's Grove. We had masters and monitors. We didn't have CCTV, they'd have probably liked that, but we were kept very much under control and very much monitored. Timings for everything were very important. It was difficult to get away. There were certain times you were allowed to walk into town or into Clifton. They immediately identified you with the brown hat with cross keys on, as being from St Peter's which was a red rag to a bull to some of the local boys. You'd be very keen to get the hat off and hide it under the coat. They'd shout things or pinch your hat or make fun of the fact that you were dressed as you were. It could be embarrassing and a bit daunting when you first went into school.

Manor House, St Peter's School. Nick Banks 2nd row from front, 3rd from right (Nick Banks)

Group of boys from Manor House, St Peter's School. 1965 Nick Banks 2nd row, on far left
(Nick Banks)

When I first went, it was almost Dickensian. Discipline was paramount. You could regularly be beaten for very minor offences. If you ran down a school corridor you could get an imposition, so you had to write out a sheet of discipline procedure. If you got more of these in a set period, you'd get six of the stick. That was fairly regular. A lot of boys used to wear shorts under trousers so they had a bit more protection.

There weren't a lot of lady teachers and the lady in the sanatorium was a sister from some hospital, and was the only person that looked after you and she was what I'd call the old school, "Put on a brave face and get on with it and don't be silly". Typical stiff upper lip. Certain boys used to rebel against discipline and procedures and quite a few got away with it. We all at some stage used to rebel against things, but it was fairly soon quashed because of methods and procedures they had in place. You'd nowhere to go if you were a boarder.

You weren't allowed to go to cinemas or pubs but we used to go. We'd do bizarre things like run into town to places as far away as you could get, have two halves of mild or bitter then run back to school chewing mints all the way. There used to be the next door neighbour's wall, you could climb out of the dormitory window onto the fire escape and clamber over this wall, shimmy along for 50 metres then drop down, go to the Burton Stone and go through the same regime to get back in. But that was fraught with danger.

When the first James Bond film came out, 'Dr No', because of the weather there was no games so we'd got free time and were supposed to do extra study. An awful lot of us went to see 'Dr No' and got caught and disciplined.

You were in a dormitory but you had like a mess room. About ten boys would share one room for studying or recreation where you could listen to the radio or do any hobbies. Dormitories were six boys of similar age and an older boy would have his bed there in control of that particular room. It was freezing in winter months, just a sheet and a blanket I think. Used to go to bed with a jumper under your pyjamas to try to keep warm.

Younger boys used to do fagging. They'd go round and ring the bell at set times to wake people up. You had to get up very early to clean the prefects' study. The older boys were allowed to smoke, so ashtrays and rubbish all over. You'd have to put the milk out in mid morning break, clean it away then later on do the other messes. Then ring the bell for prayers at night after you'd done your homework. If somebody wanted a call at six o'clock in the morning, you were getting up at five or half past to deal with it.

We'd enjoy going into Clifton for a walk or up to Clifton Ings. There's a beetle called the tansy beetle, a translucent green beetle, which is only known in York and very few other places in the country. We had great fun trying to find these, bring them back and keep them in a little box in the study until they'd come out at night and go all over.

We'd meet all sorts of people, locals and fishermen down by the river. It was a good community.

We used to go out and meet girls. If we were caught we'd have been in serious problems, it wasn't acceptable. There weren't many female teachers at the school and it was very, very chauvinistic. It used to be the highlight of the year at the end of summer term when we'd have speech day. Mothers and sisters would come along, they were allowed to walk round and we could actually look at them and chat to them.

In my experience you were excluded somewhat from normal life. I wasn't because I was a bit of a rebel but I think an awful lot of them were really sheltered and I don't think they were in the real world. We did have good times, I did enjoy some of the time but it was my personal circumstances, I felt it was probably not appropriate for me. As a result I was glad to leave.

Several years ago there was an enquiry concerning the intended closure of a public lane.

Opposite the Burton Stone pub there was a walkway that went through the main fabric of St Peter's and down between the two playing fields, the cricket ground and rugby ground, to the bottom of Love Lane that went down to Queen Anne's and then round into The Avenue. And one went a bit further on and came down at the river, part of St Peter's boathouse. We used to have local lads come and make fun of us when we were in our shorts playing rugby or cricket because they could stand on the public footpath and shout abuse or make fun of us, or girls would wolf whistle. After I left they had problems with vandalism and with people exercising dogs on the school playing fields, as a result of being able to walk through, and then people just wandering round the school campus. It became a security issue. Obviously the school was concerned about the safety of the pupils as well as health and safety for the area.

The residents didn't like it but St Peter's had actually taken on Queen Anne's campus and joined it altogether. There was one walkway that would take people down to the river but of course there's other walkways so all they had to do was go down The Avenue and cut round the back.

Gerald Barker recalls this,

There was quite a petition, one or two people felt very strongly about it and the architect chap in Clifton, he acted virtually on behalf of the community against the school. They had a conference about it. It went on for several days at the Guildhall. They felt it should be open, it was built with that in mind, but the school put such a strong case, that it came down against the community and for the school.

But the locals tend to get on with the school most of the time. Gerald and one or two others,

have regular meetings with the headmaster. It's really to do with what the school was up to and how it's fitting in with our lives here. I think the only thing that upset me after I got here was the building of the sports hall. We did have quite a battle with that. On the other hand, they had a tree taken down earlier this year and now we get this lovely view of the school which we didn't used to have. The school is quite powerful and it pays a lot in local authority taxes and is beneficial to the community.

– Chapter 11 –
LUMLEY BARRACKS

Lumley Barracks 1994 (Van Wilson)

Lumley Barracks in Burton Stone Lane was built in 1911, designed by W H Brierley, with a coat of arms in the Coalbrookdale Royal Arms design. It became the premises for HQ, Battery and the Ammunition Column of the West Riding Royal Garrison Artillery Volunteers, and the Yorkshire Hussars. The barracks was named after the Lumley family and was officially opened on 14th November by Mrs Constance Ellinor Lumley, wife of Colonel (later Brigadier General), the Honourable Osbert Victor George Athling Lumley, Colonel in Charge of the Yorkshire Hussars, third son of Richard George Lumley, 9th Earl of Scarborough.

In the 1920s the TA (Territorial Army) Artillery 54th (West Riding and Staffordshire) Medium Brigade was based there, commanded by Lt Colonel H Stead. Major Innes Ware (later the city coroner), commanded the 213th Medium Battery. The barracks continued as the base for the TA army reserve force, as well as for cadets aged 14-18. Army regulars were stationed there during the Second World War, and members of the TA were called up for war service.

Colin Carr was born in 1942. He recalls,

Originally at Lumley Barracks it was the Yorkshire Hussars, then in the mid 1950s their title was changed to the Queen's Own Yorkshire Yeomanry. The Yorkshire Hussars were equipped with Daimler scout cars. I remember eight at the garage. They could drive up to 60 miles an hour. They'd be reconnaissance squadron. They'd go out on a weekend, sometimes you'd see them on Malton Road in convoy. [In their training] *they'd go ahead of the main force, a mile away from*

Daimler Scout car used by Yorkshire Hussars (Colin Carr)

the enemy, shut the engines off, go forward and assess the enemy, what strength they were, if they had any tanks. So they were the eyes of the unit. The main sections in the army are the infantry, mounted troops, artillery and the services, to bring food, ammunition and supplies. We did four subjects. Drill first of all, drill without a rifle. You did rifle drill later when you'd passed part one. Basic drill, map reading, weapon training and field craft were the main things they taught you. You'd get shouted at. But you'd get boisterous lads, they were hard to handle and they got cheeky. It was difficult to stop them. Bill Powell was a sergeant major, he'd soon tell them. He was an ex regular. He put them in their place.

Most blokes join the TA because they're interested in the army. It's very strict for basic training then after that it's a bit more lax. You've been taught to do what you have to do in the event of war. In the Second World War the TA officers were usually too old for military service. They'd probably been in the First World War and were maybe 50 or 60 years old. So they were with the cadets and the Home Guard.

The Air Training Corps was also based at Lumley Barracks.

They didn't allow girls in the Air Training Corps then. So they formed a similar unit, the Girls' Training Corps, and they were taught a bit of aircraft recognition and things like that. They used to join in the training sometimes with the Air Training Corps although they weren't part of it. [Girls were not allowed to join the ATC squadron until 1984].

I was interested in the army from a very young age. When I was 14, I'd heard there was a cadet unit on Lumley Barracks. It was the 5th Battalion West Yorkshire regiment army cadet force. And I was with them for five months and I still wasn't issued with a uniform so I discovered a new cadet unit, REME, Royal Electrical and Mechanical Engineers, at Tower Street Drill Hall. And I joined them instead until 1960. When you were 18 you had to leave the cadets in the hopes you

*would join the army or go in the TA. I was a drummer bugler in the
Corps of Drums from 1960 to 1964.*

REME patrol. Colin Carr on left (Colin Carr)

On the 1st April 1967 all the Yorkshire TA regiments, including the 3rd
Battalion Prince of Wales's own Regiment in Yorkshire, became the
Yorkshire Volunteers. At this time the site at Lumley Barracks consisted
of the hut for D Company West Yorkshire cadets, a hut for Intelligence
Corps, (who seemed to be invisible to everyone else), buildings housing
the TA, the military police unit who trained on Clifton Aerodrome, the
quartermaster's stores which contained equipment for a few cadet units
in the city, offices, the married quarters for soldiers at Fulford, the small
REME garage where the Scammell truck was housed, and a vehicle ramp
and pit. At the same time 110 Squadron of the Air Training Corps, which
had been based at Archbishop Holgate's Grammar School, moved to
Lumley Barracks, leaving the school with 116 Squadron. In 1968 Colin

joined the Yorkshire Volunteers TA at Lumley Barracks. I got 18s 6d for a day's training. Probably the officers would get a bit more. Parade night would be a Tuesday night from half past seven till half past nine. Then you used to have weekends away. The Royal Army Service Corps transport column used the large brick building at the barracks with the drill hall and kept their vehicles in a row of garages. They had a large American truck called a Diamond T. They were better than the British trucks. The army cadets had a dozen 303 Lee Enfield rifles, they were chained up. They probably took the bolts out and put them in a safe. The 2-2 rifle range was built later. It's a smaller calibre than a proper rifle that the army use, just like an air gun, training cadets to be good shots. At camps they used to have guard mounting competitions. There's about ten in a guard. Each unit would produce ten smart cadets and you'd mount a guard. During the night you have to have a guard in case of incidents, fire or being attacked by the enemy. So you'd do a parade outside the guard room, stand to attention with a rifle, and an officer would

USA army truck (Colin Carr)

inspect you. He'd pass the guard, 'all smart enough', you'd get dismissed, go into the guard room and do two hours on and four off during the night. You did it on rotation. But you never got a good sleep, always somebody talking. It was an offence to fall asleep while on guard. You'd get really into trouble.

In 1969 they decided to have a Corps of Drums at Lumley Barracks and they asked me to teach the drummers and buglers. Typical army, they didn't ask for volunteers. So I had to teach reluctant recruits. I was given the rank of honorary Lance Corporal. Some were interested, about half a dozen, but the others didn't want to do it. I did get them together and they could march round the barracks playing solos and repeats.

Colin was an instructor in the Sea Cadets for some years but in 1983 he became a civilian instructor and Adult Warrant Officer, and he

went along to the Air Training Corps and asked the CO if he'd like me to form a band. Although he thought it was a good idea,

the squadron civilian committee weren't prepared to take the risk of buying instruments only to see the venture fail. So I set to and made six drums out of old chemical drums from work, with clothes lines and hoops I scrounged from central barracks. Then I told them I could now provide equipment and would be able to form a band without any cost to the unit. But if the band were successful, I would then expect the committee to spend money to replace the home made drums. At that time the squadron had a new CO, Flight Lieutenant Boyle, and he welcomed the idea. So with my home made

Colin Carr and home made drums. 110 Squadron ATC (Colin Carr)

181

Colin Carr with tenor drum at Lumley Barracks (Colin Carr)

drums I formed the band. It was a drum and bugle band at first and then eventually became a drum and flute band. They joined because they wanted to do it. There's nothing more fulfilling than teaching people who are interested. They couldn't learn enough. I was Band Master for the next six years.

They had leg aprons made of leather, or some of the bands had fur ones. The regiments that served in Africa had lion skins and the ones that served in India had leopard skins. Your drums rub on your knee, they used to wear your trousers out. And you wore ammunition boots and had gaiters and straps. There were three different sizes of drums. The front row had snare drums and they went rat-a-tat-tat. The bass drum, you had to have a big lad carrying that, he kept the beat, so you kept in step. And tenor drums which didn't have a snare on. Those with the tenor drums used to spin their sticks, they didn't play a lot.

Bill Powell commanded the army cadets. He was my CO. Eventually when I left t.e air cadets band [in 1989], *he took over as bandmaster.*

There have been several name changes in the ensuing years. In 1980, the buildings were occupied by the Prince of Wales's Own army cadets, the Air Training Corps cadets, the Yorkshire Volunteers Corps of Drums, the drill hall, a garage for the land rover and three tonners, 2.3 rifle range, and the offices and stores. The intelligence corps and married quarters remained.

In the late 1990s the old wartime huts were demolished and new purpose built headquarters were built for the army and air cadets. In 1991 at the

Officers of D Company, the West Yorkshire Regiment, Army Cadet Force.
L to R – Sgt Major Bill Powell, Sgt Major Bob Wilson, Major Lunn, (C.O.), Captain Taylor the
Adjutant (Colin Carr)

50th Anniversary parade, Bill Powell was awarded a Commandant's Certificate of Good Service for his work with the band. He retired in 2001 and died in 2010. In 2000 part of the site was sold off, the drill hall and other buildings demolished and Grosvenor Park was built.

At this time York Archaeological Trust conducted a desk top archaeological survey, edited by David Brinklow, as there was conjecture that a Roman road might lay beneath the barracks site. Their findings concluded that,

The possibility that archaeological remains of Roman date
associated with the Roman road from York (Eboracum) to Catterick
(Cataractonium) might be encountered was identified. The antiquity
of Burton Stone Lane was also determined together with the
possibility of survival of medieval archaeological deposits.

There are no records of Roman material from the present site, or in the immediate vicinity, but the main Roman road out of the fortress leading to the north lies about 250 metres to the south-west and burials are known to occur alongside this road from close to the fortress to beyond Clifton Green. A group of second century cremation burials was discovered close to the junction of Clifton and Burton Stone Lane and the extent of this cemetery is uncertain. It is possible that outlying burials belonging to this cemetery may exist on the site. The site does, however, have archaeological potential since it lies immediately adjacent to Burton Stone Lane which is known to have been in regular use from at least the 13th or 14th century up to the present day.

The barracks is now the Duncombe Barracks, comprising the Lumley Detachment Army Cadet Force, and the 110 City of York Squadron Air Training Corps. On 30th July 2008 the cadet force received an Agreement of Affiliation with the Royal British Legion.

Lumley Road 1994 (Van Wilson)

– Chapter 12 –
CLIFTON AERODROME AND
THE SECOND WORLD WAR

Sir Alan Cobham, a pilot with the Royal Flying Corps in the First World War, and later a test pilot, became a pioneer of long distance aviation after the war. His team of 14 aircraft toured the country, giving air displays. They came to York in 1933.

Opening of York Municipal Aerodrome 1936

Henry King was born in York in 1917. He worked at Croft's hairdresser's and tobacconists in High Ousegate, as an apprentice, including one day a week on a stall at the cattle market. But he longed to fly.

Sir Alan Cobham used to have an air circus. They'd take passengers up for aerobatic flights, looping the loop. I was interested in aircraft and he was marvellous. So I saved up 7s 6d, fortunately we got quite a few tips, so that I could have a flight. Then I joined York Flying Club and got an odd flying lesson. Commander Croxford was the chief instructor and he took a liking to me and a fellow called Morrison because we hadn't much money. My mother lent me £30. I had to pay her back so much a week. I was the youngest man at the aerodrome to go solo. It was only through the kindness of Commander Croxford. Bob Morrison and I used to share our flying time, I'd navigate for him and he'd navigate for me. We always got lost. You had no wireless, it was all barnstorming. We used to fly by the Bradshaw method (the railway timetable), and followed the railway lines. We'd do a few stupid things. Before the law of the southern harness, you just had a stomach belt. You dropped out of

Gypsy Moth run by Yorkshire Aviation Services 1930s. Bob Morrison in back (Yorkshire Air Museum)

the seat and were just hung in this belt. And we'd get out and stand on the wing. We'd seen Alan Cobham do it! It was something out of this world. I was the apprentice that flew over York cattle market.

In 1933 York Corporation was approached by Yorkshire Aviation Services who operated an air taxi service and flying school at Leeming. The Vale of York was seen as good flying country, the land being flat and generally offering plenty of scope for forced landings. Situated in Clifton Without and Rawcliffe was a suitable area of 163 acres. The Air Ministry granted approval after a site visit in 1934. Land was purchased at a cost of £12,165 and a club house and hangar were built, and a runway 600 yards in all directions was constructed. This would be lengthened to 1000 yards.

The York Municipal Aerodrome (later known as Clifton Aerodrome) was officially opened by Viscount Swinton, Secretary of State for Air on 4th July 1936. The programme began with Tom Campbell Black leading a fleet of British Empire Air Display aircraft. The Lord Mayor took the inaugural flight. The latest civil aircraft on display included the Percival Vega Gull 'a fast and beautiful four seater, top speed over 170 mph', and the Hillson Praga, a high wing cantilever cabin monoplane.

Lord Swinton presented the Lord Mayor with a licence, which authorised the council to 'conduct an aerodrome'. Yorkshire Aviation Services was given the contract to run the club, with lessons at 40 shillings an hour, and short flights costing ten shillings. The flying club owned seven aircraft including Avro Cadet, Hornet, Gypsy Moths and Leopard Moths. After the Munich crisis, the aeroplanes were put into use as part of the Civil Air Guard, who recruited civilians and trained them to fly in case of war. Richard Harwood was one of these.

I joined the Civil Air Guard in 1938 and got my air licence. The amenities of the clubhouse were good. You could have lunch or dinner and the rate of flying was down to ten shillings an hour. It took the average person 12-15 hours before they went solo. Because of the subsidising, you had to sign something, that if anything did happen, you would volunteer.

Richard did move on to join the RAF. He returned to York in 1942 after the Baedeker air raid.

When the Germans bombed York, my father's glass and china shop in Bootham was flattened. There was a glass showcase that was completely smashed, apart from one small glass shelf and in the corner was a Royal Doulton figure of Mr Churchill.

16hp Super Snipe fire tender touring car and trailer at aerodrome (Yorkshire Air Museum)

Gerald Barker and his friends would,

Wander up there and get as near to things as we could, I remember the Gypsy Moth and Tiger Moth, both biplanes. Anything that flew, in particular the pre-war aircraft were of interest. The war came on, the whole thing changed. I remember there being 50 Lysanders on the aerodrome, more of a reconnaissance aircraft than an aggressive aircraft.

By the middle of 1939, the airfield and aircraft were requisitioned by the Royal Air Force. There were no living quarters so airmen were billeted in the area. In the Spring of 1940 the Air Ministry began to fully develop the airfield, erecting more buildings. There were Whitley bombers from 51 Squadron and later Number 4 Squadron from Linton arrived with their Lysander aircraft. Other squadrons were based there temporarily over the next few years. Three runways were built in 1941-2, taking up Clifton Moor and the open land in Rawcliffe, as the airfield became a relief landing ground for Linton on Ouse. Accommodation was built for 500 personnel.

Because of the large numbers of Halifax four engined-bombers based in Yorkshire, the Ministry decided to establish a Civilian Repair Unit at Clifton. Two large hangar complexes were built, one at the Rawcliffe village side, the other at Water Lane. During the remainder of the war over 2,000 Halifax aircraft were repaired and nearly 3,000 employees worked there, mostly women, a lot working as riveters and patching shell holes on the fuselages.

The planes were brought in trucks to the hangar, some spattered with blood and in quite a mess. Some, which returned from the Middle East, had to be de-sanded because the planes got so clogged with sand. Some had been hit by enemy anti aircraft fire, others had been attacked by fighters and many had crashed while returning from raids. When the work had been completed each bomber was given an air test and then flown back to its home airfield. Some members of the Air Transport Auxiliary flew the repaired planes out, including Lettice Curtis, the first woman to fly four engined bombers. The entire operation was controlled by Handley Page, the company that made the Halifax. Sir Frederick Handley Page would visit occasionally.

Margaret Arnold lived at the Bumper Castle pub, close to the aerodrome, and would often go to play there during the war.

You could go through where they kept ammunition and things.
Mounds of earth with tunnels in, we'd dare one another to run

through in the dark. We climbed onto the aeroplanes. They were working on them, I'd go in the front and pretend I was a pilot. I remember going up in a little aeroplane. Somebody coming and saying, would we like a ride. And going across Bumper, waving to my mother and father as they were holding their breath, coming back and saying, "It's lovely from the air, you see how it's been done, roundabouts and streets. The pattern was lovely".

Margaret Inns and Colin Fearn at York Aerodrome c1940 (Margaret Arnold née Inns)

She recalls how it had changed when she had a family of her own.

No houses on the aerodrome, of course, even when we first came in '61. We'd take our pram along Green Lane, with big holes in the road. We could take our dog right across the aerodrome. It was all country, lovely really.

Roy Hodgson was born in 1935.

My family lived at Moor Farm, Water Lane, about half a mile from Rawcliffe Drive.

Bumper Castle Lane was only a very minor road, it wasn't tarmacced until well into the '30s and our farm bordered onto it. There'd be about 35 acres on the south side of the lane, and on the other side, another 20 acres. We had cows mainly, pigs, and hens and geese. I had about 30 rabbits. Before the war we just had hayfields, and a herd of about 25 Friesian cows.

The farm was very basic, we had no mains water, no electricity, the water was taken from a subterranean stream about 60 foot down and pumped up with a very old single cylinder. We had one tap in the yard and that was our water supply. The airfield was at the end of our garden, just a large grass field, no runways or anything then. They built the clubhouse at the end of Rawcliffe Lane. With being in the Model Aircraft Society we used to use the airfield for flying model planes. I flew once to Woodford near Manchester in an Auster three seater. I also flew in a Tiger Moth doing stunts over the airfield which was quite exciting, I was about 14.

I used to spend a lot of my time on the farm. I'd ride ponies and it was like a ranch style life. I'd help with the milking and cleaning the cows out, bringing the cows in. We had quite a lot of tame pigeons, there was a pigeon cote. The farm had about six horse boxes. We kept mainly riding horses not carthorses. We had to be up at six in the morning. It was all school and work. No radios, and we used paraffin lamps. They gave a good light. We didn't get electricity till the '70s.

In 1939 the Air Ministry came and said they wanted to enlarge the airfield. It was only 600 acres previously, purchased from three of our neighbour farmers, Mr Plummer, Mr Holmes on Shipton Road and Mr Clemenson at Rawcliffe. That was the nucleus of the airfield in the 1930s. We were given two weeks notice. We had to get all the furniture out, stored a lot of it in the farm buildings, had to go and live on Shipton Road with my grandma. We got the land for the bungalows back but the compensation was £350, didn't get that until 1960.

The airfield took all the land on the north side of Bumper Castle Lane, they put proper standard runways in and it doubled its size. But the ground was too soft for the aircraft, they were all right as long as they stayed on the runway but if they went off, they tended to sink into the ground. So they decided to make it a maintenance airfield, and all the planes shot up over Germany were flown in for repairs. And then they built more hangars at Rawcliffe. It became Monroe's [later Armstrong Patent's] shock absorber factory after the war. Just adjacent to our fields where the Backies are, there was a big cookhouse, and the WAAF camp was on Water Lane.

Where the gypsy site is now, there was a big concrete apron on the airfield. The planes would assemble there and trundle across the

Walter Raymond Hodgson and Blanche Hodgson, parents of Roy. Mid 1930s, Moor Farm, Water Lane (Roy Hodgson)

road. There were some sliding gates across Green Lane and into the hangars, and they'd bring them out in the mornings about six o'clock, rev up the engines, wake us all up and they were flown off back to the air bases.

The airfield was badly damaged in the Baedeker raid on York in April 1942. The guard room received a direct hit.

After the raid, they brought some anti aircraft equipment, four or five rocket launching devices, 38 barrels on each one. Two or three months after the big raid, a German plane went over and they fired every one of these rocket launchers, and shot it down. The noise was phenomenal. They never fired them anymore. I don't think there was a need.

Roy Hodgson 1950s (Roy Hodgson)

We had a big happening when a hangar caught fire. The fire brigade came immediately, they emptied our pond in about 20 minutes. But they had to get hoses from the hydrants in Rawcliffe Drive. The whole thing was melting to the ground, it was so hot. [This disaster occurred in 1943 when nine Halifaxes were destroyed after a spark ignited petrol and three hangars were burned out].

[After the war] *my grandma sold the land, she kept an interest in some of the land, and allowed her two sons to use it. When she died, they sold it for building land and English Heritage said they had to take aerial pictures. There was a Roman camp, so they wouldn't let him sell six acres of the land. It's still there as a field now, you can get access to it by the Mercedes garage. They wanted them to keep the farm as it was because it was a typical 1850s style building, a double farmhouse with a valley roof.* [But because it needed new floors, walls and roof], *they decided they would rebuild it in the same style. They've even put the chimneys on. They've got minstrel galleries in, and the pigsty is converted into a dormer bungalow, the old cow stable is converted into a cottage. They've still got the original round window in the building, and the original sandstone coping on the roof. It's quite interesting. The airfield was rough ground in its day, it did provide good habitat for wildlife. At least 20 or 30 pairs of skylarks on there, and lots of hares and rabbits. They all went of course when they started developing it.*

After the war nearly 1000 Halifaxes went to Clifton to be broken up. A huge pile of metal over 80 feet high could be seen near Rawcliffe village. The RAF left the site in 1946. The buildings near the main entrance were loaned to the army for offices and for storing army pay records. The Water Lane hangar complex was used for storing Home Office equipment.

Guy Jefferson was born in 1928. After visiting Linton on Ouse as a child he began a lifelong interest in aviation. He enlisted in the RAF at 17 as ground crew, and stayed at RAF Linton as a radio/radar engineer.

York airfield was all grass in those days, no runways at all. It was there I had the first taste of flying. They had some sort of open day. There was a privately owned Domineer, the pilot used to sit in front, you would be behind. Cost me ten shillings, equivalent of about £50 today for this ride, but it was worth it. A girl was flying it, I was amazed.

Guy Jefferson 2010 (Van Wilson)

We took off to the west and went round by the hospital. I had my camera and I clicked the thing and she jumped, "What the hell's that?" On that same day, on the programme was an item, 'How not to fly an aeroplane'. Along came this aeroplane from Brough, from the Blackburn aircraft company. He was throwing this thing round at real low level. He had some guts, doing everything he shouldn't do. All of a sudden, he misjudged the site and crashed right in front of us and broke his arms. That set me off for flying, I couldn't get enough of it. I joined the Observer Corps so I could go flying in big aeroplanes like Hastings and Dakotas. I was a chief observer.

Guy later flew with Sherburn Flying Club.

Anyone in the Air Force is entitled to be a social member of the club, so I was made a Bomber Baron. We have our own tie and everything.

Halifax aircraft over the York area during World War Two (Van Wilson)

Guy remembers the pile of broken up Halifaxes after the war.

The hangars were called MAP hangars, Ministry of Aircraft Production. There was one T2 hangar there, the only one the RAF had.

As you went down the A19, you could see this huge pile of broken bombers. You've never seen so many carcases of aeroplanes. There used to be a farm down there, that has all gone, it is the Backies now.

When Guy got married, he lived off Shipton Road and saw the development of the airfield as it gradually happened.

I used to walk along the old runway with my dog. Every day I went along there was foundations going up. In 1970, a Vampire aircraft landed by mistake on York airfield. So I went on my little scooter, got into this Vampire and I called up Rufforth. He was from an airfield in Lincoln and this was his first solo and he thought that York Minster was Lincoln Cathedral. He towed round and he saw York airfield and decided to land. By that time York airfield had barbed wire and posts. He managed to leapfrog this fence across the runway and he'd had the sense to taxi back to the control tower, which was still there. He sent a message to Linton that his radio had failed so that's why I came into it. We got it fuelled up again and I said to this pilot, "You can't get onto t'runway now, it's impossible, this guy's leapfrogged a fence to land it here". I was stood at the control tower. He was going quite fast, he went past me, heading straight for Byron Drive near where the library is now. What the people on Byron Drive must have thought, to see this Vampire only about ten feet above the chimney pots! But he got away and got it back to Linton.

Guy was given permission to fly his models on the airfield. His models are much admired. Some of them, like the Lysander and Whitley bomber, now hang in the NAAFI at the Yorkshire Air Museum.

I designed my own aeroplanes and I used to fly them. I built from scratch, didn't have a plan. I worked from silhouettes out of books, scaled it up to 72 inch wing span. I had gliders on there and the Knavesmire.

My job at Linton was to repair radio and radar, anything to do with electronics. They got so reliable that they hardly ever broke down. So in my spare time, I used to think, "I could make his job easier", by doing this, that and the other.

Guy Jefferson receives British Empire Medal (Guy Jefferson)

Guy came up with a number of inventions throughout his career. The most important was probably the Ultrasonic Undercarriage Position Indicator, a device which acted as a safety break and which is still used on modern aircraft. This saved lives and saved aircraft. For his services to radio and radar communications, he was awarded the British Empire Medal.

In 1949 York Flying Club was formed, but the small number of members could not afford the high rent of the airfield. In spite

PRICE 1/- N⁰ 3977

AIR DISPLAY

ORGANISING COMMITTEE IN ASSOCIATION WITH
YORK FESTIVAL COMMITTEE

CLIFTON AERODROME

YORK

16th 17th JUNE 1951

Telephone: YORK 54384

Air Display 1951

Clifton Aerodrome Memorial at Kettlestring Lane unveiled by Richard Harwood (Oliver Bostock)

of holding a successful fund raising air display in 1951, it closed in 1953. The Water Lane hangars were retained as Ministry of Agriculture grain stores. The Government sold the airfield in 1955 to York Corporation for housing. By the 1970s, most of the buildings had gone and part of the site was used as a golf driving range. Over the years following the war, the aerodrome made a wonderful playground for local children with a lot of imagination.

THE BACKIES

Clifton Backies, which was part of the airfield, was designated a local nature reserve in 2002 because of its diversity of wildlife and its potential for education. After the war it had fallen into disrepair and became overgrown. The Friends of Clifton Backies was founded. By not using artificial weed killers, the area has developed naturally and incorporates unimproved pasture, scrub woodland and hay meadow. It provides a habitat for voles, rabbits, foxes, shrews, mice, hedgehogs, weasels and even deer.

Doug Heald, who lived in Burton Stone Lane, enjoyed playing there.

The name came about because we used to say 'over the back gardens'. They were fields that hadn't been put into any use, remnants of allotments from the war years. Towards where the Burdyke beck runs along, you had a military camp. We'd go there and find ˅˅ ˅˅rts of artefacts. It was a wonderful play area for kids, all the shelters and bunkers. There were hydrant reservoirs, which we'd build rafts and float on. We'd go fishing with sticklebacks in the beck. The industrial part of Clifton Moor was the airfield, and towards the beck side, is now just bushland. The buildings were empty and decaying but wonderful for climbing about. It was a vast area of moorland, an open theatre of sky and fields. My father built a fence with a gate at the back [in our garden] *so you just went out and you were in the fields. I got this early interest in wildlife and flowers. We'd have small gangs, six or seven lads, on hot summer days, dressed up as Indians in warpaint, and our arrows, the ends would be wired to give them balance, quite lethal things! You stayed out till dusk, your parents didn't worry, they knew you'd be back for supper.*

I've gone to The Backies all my life. It's one of the very few remnants where it's untouched. It's good that it's managed, because people who are professional know how to bring back the habitat, but I still want that derelictness and there's not many places in the UK where you can get that, where nature does its own thing and humans are a secondary thing.

Lake at Backies 2010 (Mike Race)

Clifton Backies sign (Mike Race)

Gill May recalls a coronation party

on the aerodrome, 1953. People from all over that area came. I went as the Queen of Hearts. My mother made a pinny out of an old dressing table runner, with all these hearts, and a tray with supposedly jam tarts on it.

Peter Willow lived in Rawcliffe Lane and played on the aerodrome.

It was derelict and the buildings were dilapidated. The watch tower was still there, and every now and then the Civil Defence would come and use me and my friends to practise on. They'd put us on a stretcher and lower us down from the roof. It was exciting. There was an outside ladder hanging off the side, it would rattle when you went up there. Very occasionally a little single-engined red aeroplane would land and people would come out and look at it. Also the army would come and set tents up on there and practise manoeuvres occasionally.

Gill May at Coronation Party on Aerodrome 1953 (Gill May)

There was a man once in one of the little buildings. I think he must have been on the run. He had set himself a little home up with a tin can with holes in for a shower. He told us not to tell anyone he was there. You sensed a bit of danger, even in your naivety you knew there was something odd. There were air raid shelters, covered in grass. We used to sledge down them in winter. And some billet huts. They were very solid and they had holes for shooting out of. But sheep and cows used to go in them. Near the gate now [on Green Lane] *there's a circle where they planted flowers, and a great big building that was probably the gatehouse. It had obviously been an office.*

There were great big hangars, they said Ministry of Works. There were searchlights still, and you'd find all sorts of things, steering wheels and old aerials. The holes at the side of the runway where the landing lights had been had just been left. My friend found a pop bottle, we wondered what was in it and we were shaking it up. It went in his eye and he had to go to hospital. It was acid. When I got home all the front of my jeans was burnt. There was a little pond which had sloping sides, you had to climb over a fence to get in. I think it was for testing rubber dinghies for the Halifax.

The local policeman would come riding down and tell you to get off. I remember him telling me off for having my air gun. I'd actually paid 2s 6d for a licence. We didn't shoot birds, it was exciting shooting tin cans. You could find lots of things from World War 2, lots of bullets, and clips. I remember once we trapped a bullet, put it under a brick and shot at the back of it. Eventually we hit it and it went off with such an explosion that everybody came out. We were as amazed as they were. We had a 303 army rifle bullet. I remember a friend of mine found this 2.2 poaching gun and it came apart in two pieces with an old screw underneath. It was a Winchester and it said 1901 on it. We found it in this farmhouse and eventually it went bang and cut his hand and my head.

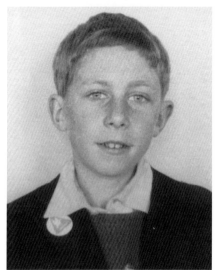

Articles from the 1950s mention how there were many unauthorised firearms about in the years after the war, which men had taken home as souvenirs. On one occasion 47 firearms were handed in to York police after the Home Secretary appealed for weapons to be surrendered. The police thought this was just the tip of the iceberg.

We played on the Ings. When the river had flooded, fish would go into

Peter Willow 1960s (Peter Willow)

Willow Row, a narrow inland water. We made rafts on the river with oil drums from Armstrong's tip. And we'd go to Ings Garage on Shipton Road with a pint [milk] bottle and six pence, and you could get a pint of two stroke petrol for our BSA Bantam. The man who served us had this little machine with a handle on the side, he'd pump it out and say, "You'll get me shot, serving petrol in a milk bottle". We'd pour it in the BSA Bantam and tear up and down, could play all afternoon on a pint of two stroke petrol. BSA Bantams were old things from the '50s. They'd be outside people's houses rusting away and they'd give us them and we'd get them going. Probably a bit missing off them, mudguards, maybe only had one brake but good enough to go on the aerodrome with.

There was a lot of wildlife there. Not so far from Bumper Castle, there were three types of newts in that pond. Sometimes girls would come and they daren't put worms on the hooks so they put fruit gums on. We put the newts in a jam jar, looked at them and then teemed them back in. I once caught a seven inch pike with a wire rabbit snare.

The aerodrome is a vast place, covered a lot of ground extending into Rawcliffe Village. There was a farmhouse at either end and a tiny little house was a shop. There were gas masks in one of the wash houses still. I remember people coming back with rabbits they'd caught to bring home for their dinner. There was a water pump in the village and a little church in a community hut, that was our youth club as well. And there was a caravan site there. We'd be gone for the day with our dogs. It was the end of an era, the end of the aerodrome.

Pam Young lives on what was the airfield.

It was all green fields. There were the grain stores up towards Tesco. They've been dismantled. A lot of people used to walk their dogs over there. There was no roundabout, now there's a horrendous amount of traffic. You were in the countryside. Now it's just houses all around.

By 2006, all the hangars had been demolished. Now there is hardly any evidence of the airfield, except for the pub named the Flying Legends, and the streets on Clifton Moor which are named after Second World War aircraft and personalities such as Amy Johnson Way, Audax Road, Lysander Close, Halifax Court and Whitley Close.

THE SECOND WORLD WAR IN CLIFTON

During the war, there were five public air raid shelters in Clifton. The biggest one at Bootham Grange, opposite Bootham Crescent, held 233 people. The others were at the football ground in Bootham Crescent, Burton Stone Lane near Glencoe Street, 50 Clifton next to the cinema, and Clifton Green itself. The head air raid warden was Colonel Innes Ware of St Peter's Grove. The York telephone manager's office in Clifton had a 'protected room' which was covered 24 hours a day and air raid warnings were filtered through a special switchboard although the warnings did not come on time in the 1942 air raid.

There were only two raids on Clifton. The first, in April 1941, only affected the Ings and there was virtually no damage. The main air raid was the Baedeker Raid. In the early hours of the morning of 29th April 1942, 84 tons of bombs were dropped on the city. There were 92 civilians killed as well as military personnel at the aerodrome. Much of the city centre was damaged and Clifton was badly affected. Queen Anne's Road, Sycamore Terrace, St Peter's School, Burton Stone Lane, The Avenue, Pickering Terrace, Westminster Road, Bootham Crescent, Avenue Terrace, Water End, Greencliffe Gardens (later Drive), Clifton Ings and Clifton itself were hit. Houses were demolished and people were trapped in many of the streets, with civil defence workers digging for hours to free them. A crater in Westminster Road was 30 yards across and 30 feet deep, another crater nearby disrupted water and gas mains.

A house in Bootham Crescent was used as a reception centre for the wounded. Dogs and cats were seen fleeing down the main road, and one lady's dog turned up under a bed at Fairfield Sanatorium on Shipton Road. (For more details about the Baedeker Raid and the home front during the war, see my book 'Ration, Raids and Romance; York During the Second World War').

Lena Mills was born in 1920. She was one of two female air raid wardens in Clifton.

I was an ARP warden. We were stationed in what was the New Lendal Chapel, [in Burton Stone Lane]. *We'd to go out on a purple* [purple alarm which meant air raid]. *We'd patrol quite a lot. On the* [night of] *the Blitz, the other girl didn't turn in. The doors shook and the place shook. It was a night was that, we don't want another one like it. I had to take some people into Sycamore Terrace". I shall never forget it because when we went to Grosvenor Terrace, the block was on fire and I thought, "How am I going to get them past this?"*

The White House, Clifton during Second World War. Note white rings round tree in foreground for the blackout

We went down Sycamore Terrace [to a first aid centre] *and first
person they clapped eyes on was their relative, he'd got a cut on his
head. The lad said to me, "I can't get over it, the way you got them
through there". But that was just part of my warden's job.*

Pauline Wright was a child living off Burton Stone Lane.

*I was frightened sometimes but I was too young to be terrified. My
father had to go out when the air raids were on* [he was a warden],
and we were on our own the night of the big raid. Every night she
[mother] *had a black bag and she used to pack a flask, a few sweets,
and comics. You couldn't have a sweet until you'd been in the shelter
an hour because they were rationed. And a little camp bed. My father
had rigged up some lighting and heating for us. I went to sleep in my
little siren suit.*

*In front of our house was a chapel and next to it was allotments and
they built air raid shelters on the allotments. The chapel was turned
into a rest centre. Every Monday afternoon my mother and her
colleagues went and saw that everything was in order because they
were given rations of tea and sugar. On the night of the raid, as the
all clear went, we ran across. There was soot all over, and my mother
said, "Come on, we've got to get there, we're needed". And there
was a family running with a new baby that had just been born in
Pickering Terrace, and every house on that street was bombed. People
came from all round. I went round carrying cups of tea. There were
WVS, everybody helped out. We had clothes,* [for people who] *came
in their night clothes. The important thing was getting people tea and
just calming them really. They had to stay there all night.*

*The next day people sorted things out, if they could go to relatives or
friends. Some houses you could go back to. I remember going round
the street with a plate and a cup, knocking on doors asking people,
could they give a spoonful of sugar, or a spoonful of tea or a scraping
of butter because everything was rationed. I remember the authorities
telling my mother off because she'd let the men and women be in the*

same room instead of dividing them.

There was an unexploded bomb in Baker Street. This area got it quite badly because the planes came along the railway line. For many years afterwards all down Grosvenor Terrace and Scarborough Terrace, you could see where the incendiaries had dropped on the pavement, the scarring. And bullet holes on the wall at the side of the railway. I suppose it made a big impression on me as a six year old.

Marion Tweedy recalls

In Ousecliffe Gardens, the trees sheltered us a lot. I know there was some shrapnel in my bedroom chair. And all the windows went. People got killed near us, the Miss Cherrys. [This was Frances and Emily Cherry, aged 79 and 77, who lived at 18 Westminster Road]. *They laid them in the hedge bottom. We were going for a look and we were told, "No", by the police. Quite a few houses were rebuilt in Westminster Road.*

Marion Tweedy's family,

had soldiers to visit. We used to have one soldier come for his lunch quite regularly, Ronald Searle. Since then there's been the cartoonist and I often wondered, "Was it him?" He was a nice man. [Ronald Searle the artist was in the Royal Engineers from 1939 to 1942, so he may have been in York as the Royal Engineers had their headquarters here].

When the war ended, one lady described walking down Rawcliffe Lane, which had flags and bunting hung out. After being used to the blackout, she was particularly struck by the different coloured curtains and the rooms lit up so that 'it resembled fairy lights. It was wonderful'.

Street party in 1945 off Burton Stone Lane (Eileen Race)

– Chapter 13 –
SHOPS AND BUSINESSES

Before the Second World War, Clifton was still very much a village, with everything that the residents needed within reach. For a bit more variety, there was also Bootham at close hand. As times changed and people began to shop further afield, preferring to drive to big supermarkets where they could get most things at the same time, corner shops could not compete with prices and gradually most of them closed down. With the loss of small shops, people feel that the area also lost many of its characters and some of its community spirit.

Dandy's
55-57

Bakeries
Clifton

Confectionery, Ice cream Catering

Dandy's advert (Marilyn Powell)

Of course, in the early days, before there were many shops, tradesmen would come round the streets selling their wares and this continued even after the war.

Joan Aherne recalls that

a greengrocer came round. And the milk came. He brought a horse, [and cart] and had little cups dangling on the back and they all rattled. That was for a gill or a pint. They'd ladle it out.

Pauline Wright lived in Burton Stone Lane, where the milkman

used to come round with a horse and cart. They had an agricultural show run by the Red Cross on the field off Wigginton Road. We'd go to see our milkman's horse being dressed, part of the parade. It was a nice day out, take a picnic, there were horses and cows there.

Roy Hodgson's family had a farm on what became Clifton aerodrome. They delivered milk.

You'd ladle it out when they brought their jugs out. They didn't have bottles. It was my mother really who took it in the car, we had a BSA car in them days. It was straight from the cows, into the cooling system and then out to the people, so it was quite good, efficient.

The Plummer family also delivered milk. They had a farm in Clifton and a house called Highcliffe, close to Clifton Green. The house, between 110 and 106 Clifton, has now been replaced by Highcliffe Court. Margaret Arnold knew the Plummers.

Georgie Plummer had the farm, near the Green, and they knocked it down to make a road through for all those new houses.

William Dowell also

knew the Plummers, Ken and his brothers. Their father George [grandfather of Georgie] *was quite a character. We knew him as 'bawls' on account of his loud voice. One Christmas, the story goes, he was carving the turkey, and when all the family were* [arguing], *he shouted, 'Dang you, be quiet and I'll give you all a leg!'*

CAB PROPRIETORS

William Dowell recalls Myton's cab proprietors who claimed to have the first taxi service in York. They had taken over the business of Wales & Son Carriage Works of 43 Bootham in 1883 and in 1906 amalgamated with another company, Thackeray's. By 1908 the business was at 1-2 Barker's Terrace, a small alleyway almost opposite Clifton Green.

One family well known in York, to whom we were distantly related, were George and William Myton cab proprietors [who lived in St Peter's Grove]. *The business was started by their father, and all three drove their four wheeled cabs but, as business increased, they engaged drivers or 'cabbies'. They had a cabstand opposite their office in Bootham in front of the Old Maids' Home.* [Wandesford House].

Bill Myton could be heard shouting his orders to the cabbies, 'General Rundle at Government House and hurry', or 'Mrs Lawson, Ousecliffe', etc. The business supplied the York fire brigade with horses. Quite a sight to see the grooms, each with a pair of horses, galloping from their stables in Bootham Row to the fire station, there to be yoked to the engine and escape ladders. They also kept four or more jet black Belgian horses with flowing manes and tails for hearse and carriage service. As this firm expanded with the advent of the taxicab, George drove the first one. The taxis had a rank at the station. They were taken over later when the firm became Northern Motor Utilities Ltd with garages at Walmgate Bar. [By this time, both brothers had died, George in 1902, and William in 1911 after the firm was sued for damages after an accident].

The horse drawn vehicles must have made a lovely sight.

A special treat in the summer for my mother and a maiden aunt, when they used to hire one of Myton's horse drawn vehicles, was an open landau for a country trip round the lanes near Rawcliffe and Skelton. Prior to setting out, Fairbairn, a special cabby, was requested to drive slowly and carefully. The horse could hardly do anything else as the driver was a huge man, and apart from any passengers, he was a load by himself. It was a smart turnout, highly polished coachwork, solid rubber-tyred wheels, and, on the box, Fairbairn in a silver buttoned long blue coat and a low crowned hat.

BUTCHERS

Because Clifton was originally rural, there were many farms nearby, on Water End, Shipton Road, Rawcliffe Lane and what became Water Lane, with dairies, such as the Compton Street Dairy, which sold the eggs, butter and milk, and butchers' shops which sold the meat.

Margaret Arnold's

Grandfather [Robert Lacy] *had the butcher's shop at the end of Compton Street. He did his training in the Shambles then rented a shop in Clifton. My grandmother came down from Scotland as a children's nanny in those big houses opposite the church, to a family there. She used to pay the butcher's bills and got to know my grandfather that way. I think in 1898 they were married and set up home. They had five children but two of them died at about 18 months and they ended up with three girls. The eldest was my mum, Grace Lacy.*

Ellison Terrace with Grace Lacy aged 6 (Robert Lacy's daughter) with Hetty Hudson. 1906
(Margaret Arnold daughter of Grace Lacy)

There was also a slaughterhouse in Compton Street where the beasts and sheep would be killed. Later the business was taken over by Jack Wood. In 1953 the directors were J A Wood and Mrs G E Wood. Today the butcher's shop, still at number 65a, is owned by Tony Neary. Mr Lacy moved from the butcher's into greengrocery.

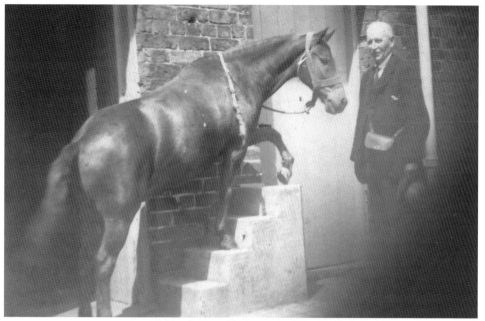

Robert Lacy and horse (Margaret Arnold)

He left in the late 1920s. They put the rent up and he said he wasn't going to pay it. And I think once or twice they did that and they accepted it and then they gave him his notice and he had to get out. He got this greengrocery round, he had a horse and cart.

They lived at number 37, at the end of Compton Street. I presume his greengrocery business was based where the pigsties were. That's where he would keep his cart and his horse. There's a row of cottages going towards Boots chemist. Before you get there, there's an alleyway and up there he had gardens, a garage and outhouse where he kept pigs. [This is now Highcliffe Court].

Because he had the garage and allotments, they were given grazing rights on the Ings, which he didn't use but he would rent it to another farmer. He had a big garden and fruit bushes. He grew a lot of things, had quite a lot of land down there, [up to] *the houses at the back of Abbey Street. Eventually he left the premises and everything to my mother and she sold it to Georgie Plummer. And the grazing rights went with it.*

NEWSAGENTS

Herbert Wilkins had shops at numbers 6 and 86 Clifton.

Derek Metcalfe recalls,

Mrs Wilkins, the newsagent, she was the daughter of Colman, [a local builder], *old Mrs Wilkins. She used to live there. I used to go in the back room and talk to her sometimes. Bloody fire up chimney, old Mrs Wilkins all bandaged legs, lovely woman. Her daughter used to manage the front.*

Malcolm Maher delivered papers for the shop.

I took papers up there, at 13, seven days a week, nights and morning. Rawcliffe Lane, Rawcliffe Avenue, Lawnswood Drive, Reighton Avenue, Melton Avenue, round top and down to Southolme Drive. Pop Storey, our headmaster, was on t'corner. He was a small bald headed fella, and he lived at top of Reighton.

The shop also sold confectionery, with paper bags folded into a cone shape, containing two ounces of aniseed balls, sherbet lemons, liquorice strings, black jacks, flying saucers, white mice or parma violets, or a sixpenny lucky bag with a few sweets and a small toy.

GROCERS

Joseph Bean's grocery store was next door but one to Wilkins' in 1932. The shop was granted a wine and spirits licence in 1938. The owner Joseph Bean died in 1948, Kathy Bean married Clarence Threlfall and the shop became Threlfall's. By the 1950s it had become a bigger concern, at 90-92 Clifton.

Clifton shops in 1930s – Bean's on left, Dandy's first shop in centre, Wilkins' newsagent's on right

Gerald Barker really liked

Bean's of Clifton, an old fashioned grocer's. People don't realise what they miss in modern times, you can go into a supermarket, you don't smell cured bacon, or ground coffee, you don't get this amalgam of smells that seemed to make the nose twitch with enthusiasm. There were hams hanging up, there was coffee ground, there was cheese cut. Occasionally you find a place in Scotland like that, but nothing much anymore. Everyone seems to think modern times are wonderful but there were simple little pleasures then, when sugar was wrapped in blue paper, and cheese cut with wire, and they used to get big pieces of butter, carve bits off, and have pats, shape it into a usable piece of butter. [Others remember bacon slicers, a quarter of loose Typhoo tea, and groceries which were not in prepacked plastic packets, but weighed and wrapped individually].

Gerald also recalls that some grocers offered a delivery service, like Cross's, originally Britton's,

at the bottom of Bootham. I remember my mother going down. She'd go and sit on a stool and give the person behind the counter an order of what she wanted. Or they would send a rep out and they would deliver. That was probably once a week.

George Britton, Grocer's, Clifton House, Bootham

As well as foodstuffs, including Robertson's marmalade, Scott's Porage Oats, and Essence of Coffee and Chicory Essence, they also stocked Lifebuoy and Wright's coal tar soap, Oxydol and Omo washing powder, and Robin starch.

In 1909, at number 22 Clifton, there was George W Windust, boot dealer, and Miss Windust selling toys, stationery and fancy goods. By 1939 the shop was Windust and March and was run by Maria Windust and Clara

March. The shop was situated next to the Old Manor House, where Petersway now stands. The children in the area would spend many an hour looking through the window at the toys they could not afford.

Pauline Wright recalls that

Clifton was a very thriving area. There was Ruddock's chemist. I think Lloyd's took it over when Mr Ruddock retired. It's now a cobbler's. And I remember there was a dark little shop [Windust]. *I think of it as a toy shop but whether it actually was, I don't know. I remember going in there and buying transfers that you licked and stuck on your hand. The post office moved to the other side near the Old Grey Mare.* [The post office has moved several times, from the right hand side of the road to the left, and it is now inside the Spar supermarket].

Marion Tweedy explains that,

What is now the cartridge shop, the Miss Windusts had that, there was two of them. I probably went in the front because there might be toys. They had a lending library in the back.

Marion also visited Gibson's and Burke's.

It's part of the Hotel Noir now [on the left of the Green]. *It was Gibson's when I was a girl, they had two daughters. Then some people called Thresh had it. It was just like someone's front room with a bay window. Gibson's had ladies' knickers hung up on strings.*

There's Abbey Street, then Highcliffe Court, then the first shop after that was Mrs Burke's, she had a post office and she always wore a beret and had her hair cut like a man. I think she sold things like socks and cotton and things of that nature.

There were smaller shops which were just confectioners or tobacconists, where you could buy two Wild Woodbines and two matches. These were often run by women. Mary Bedford was a confectioner at 3 Clifton in 1909, and Mrs Maria Oman, a grocer and newsagent at 30 Clifton in the same year. Miss Sissons of 102 Clifton, a few houses before the entrance to Abbey Street, had a small sweet shop in her front room in the 1950s and early '60s. She sold onion crisps, before the advent of cheese and onion and other flavoured crisps, and mint flavoured ice lollies.

Avenue Terrace in 1960s (York Oral History Society)

CLIFTON HARDWARE

Robert Flower started Streamline Taxis in 1937 at 88 Clifton but unfortunately the premises and cars were destroyed in the Second World War. He was also based at what was number 1 Clifton at that time. The taxi firm moved elsewhere and he opened a hardware shop called Flower's, selling the usual tools and utensils, as well as paraffin, oil lamps and hurricane lanterns. The name was changed to Clifton Hardware in 1974, two years before his death at the age of 80.

The shop was enlarged and modernised, and the Yorkshire Evening Press reported in July 1999 that new owner Neil Griffin 'likes to say yes to customers and carries 10,000 lines'. The shop is now Birdie's Perch, a card and gift shop.

Pam Young says

> *It used to be an old fashioned hardware shop like Barnitt's. You could go in and buy one screw. It was a shame when he went.*

DANDY'S

The name Dandy's is synonymous with catering in Clifton, and indeed in York. Pam Young explains

> *They were highly thought of. There were Bettys and Terry's in town, but people I've spoken to say Dandy's is on a par with them.*

Hilda Smithies was born in 1888 and came to York from Castleford, marrying John Frank (Jack) Dandy. Jack worked for Britton's grocer's in Bootham, and the Dandy family ice cream business, which began in a room in their house in Compton Street, was founded to augment his income.

Marion Tweedy recalls how people strolling by the river could cool themselves with 'Dandy Ices',

> *The end house in Compton Street, where the lane comes along* [from the river], *you could get ice creams there.*

From small beginnings, the family expanded by leasing a shop in Bootham, close to the Marygate tower, in the name of Hilda Dandy, confectioner and caterer. In 1928 they opened a shop on Clifton itself at number 30, next to the snicket leading to Lumley Road, taking over from Farmery's confectioners. This shop was in the name of Kathleen Mary Dandy, Hilda and Jack's daughter. By this time, Jack Dandy had his own grocer's shop in Nunnery Lane. The family also opened a bakehouse at 22 Burton Stone Lane in 1936. This was a large double fronted house, with a garage and rooms to use as offices. Hilda and Jack's son, Derrick, always known as Dick, became involved at this time, and trained with Beaumont's bakery in Walmgate. With the building of new estates in Kingsway and Burdyke, off Water Lane, the family opened another shop at number 49 Crichton Avenue in the 1930s to serve that community. It was managed by Hilda's sister Marie King.

Dick Dandy, recording his memories for his family, relates that

Mother was one of the first makers of ice cream in York, apart from that produced in restaurants. The making of ice cream was no easy task. The machine consisted of a metal drum which held the ice cream mixture. This was turned with a handle through bevel gearing which turned an inner 'dasher', which stirred the mixture and eased it from the sides of the drum whilst it was being frozen. An outer wooden tub was filled with chopped ice and coarse salt which was packed round the inner drum. The mixture was made

from fresh milk, boiled in a two gallon enamelled pail placed inside an outer bath of water and heated on the gas stove. Sugar and custard powder paste were added, along with Mrs D's secret ingredient, which gave the ices that 'je ne sais quoi' taste. Ice was delivered by W D Marks, hide and skin merchants, in two hundredweight blocks. These were 'put to bed' by the muscled delivery man by the use of large pincers or ice grips. The ice was interned in a dug-out in the yard and covered with Hessian sacks or sawdust to keep from melting.

Kathleen Mary and Derrick Dandy April 1933 (Marilyn Powell)

Mother decided to employ a young man named Harold Hall to sell ices from an ice cream cart. Ice cream was seasonal, so, in the winter, mother extended our range of goods to home made bread and cakes which were sold door to door by Mr Hall. A second-hand box tricycle was bought and the back kitchen or scullery was fitted with an electric oven to complement the capacity of the gas oven for this growing business empire. Electric ovens were in their infancy, heated by direct current, which made our 'currant fancies' anything but direct!

The tricycle inevitably developed punctures which were repaired by Mr Tudor who ran a cycle repair shop from the corner premises of a yard of lock up garages on the Compton Street side of the Old Grey Mare. His major skill was to rewind the armatures of magnetos but the development of coil ignition had reduced the need for this skill so he too needed to broaden the scope of his business as technology marched on. Wireless had arrived and he used to recharge the two

Kathleen Mary Dandy on right outside Dandy's in 1930s (Marilyn Powell)

volt accumulator that was necessary to drive the array of thermodic
valves in the early wireless sets, at a charge of sixpence.

During the 1930s with changes of the numbering in Clifton, number 30 became 88. In 1940 Kathleen Mary Dandy married Sid Anderson, and their daughter Marilyn, now Powell, was born in late 1941. During the Second World War, the shops were badly affected by the Blitz of 29th April 1942. The Bootham shop was demolished, but the others were rebuilt and repaired. Marilyn has family letters written after this incident.

Hilda's father George Smithies and his wife Martha were staying with Hilda and Jack at the time. On 1st of May, George wrote to his son Cyril, evoking the horrors of that night.

> *We have been blown out from Hilda's and have had to come to*
> *Winnie's* [Hilda's sister in Huntington Road]. *A big bomb dropped*
> *in the next garden but one, and all the windows and roof of Hilda's*
> *place is out, and some of the inner walls shifted. Whether the place*
> *will be condemned or not, we don't know. The Bootham shop is*
> *blown and the Clifton one nearly so. The house next to Hilda's is*
> *partly down and the next house, where the bomb dropped, completely*
> *down and four persons were killed in it. Jerry didn't half pepper us.*
> *The whole sky was hanging with chandeliers whilst the planes went*
> *backwards and forwards throwing out bombs and incendiaries.*

The next letter on the 5th May to Cyril and his wife Doris came from his sister Winnie.

> *Hitler and his friends, 20 of them, spent 1½ hours with us, dive*
> *bombing and machine gunning. All your dear relations at York are*
> *safe but nobbut just* [only just]. *Hilda has lost practically everything*
> *inside so they have all cleared out to various places.*

By June Hilda's parents were back home in Scarborough. Her father wrote to Cyril again.

We are both still dazed but mother is keeping up better than I thought she would, and now she has got home to her own way of living, she is brightening up. Nobody knows what it is like except those who have been through it. When the bombs started I put some clothes on, we both stayed in bed. The others went down into the sitting room and before many minutes, the whole window came in, shutter and all. They then rushed down into the cellar. In the meantime, we were upstairs dodging under the bedclothes every time he came over. The windows and window casings came flying in, glass flying all over the bed and sticking into the bed head. Wardrobes, which were locked, flew open, and the drawers in the chest came open. The roof of the house was all blown off and all the windows and doors smashed. Even the henhouse at the bottom of the garden was smashed to pieces but none of the hens killed. Although Hilda is spending part of the day in the house, no-one is sleeping in it. It is uncertain whether it can be repaired. They have got the bakehouse working and also the Clifton and Crichton shops. They have now got the roof on and Jack sleeps in the house sometimes and he could probably arrange to put you up, if you could catch him in before he goes out to his bowling green.

After the war, the family moved over the road to a bigger shop at 55-57 Clifton, leaving number 88 to become a hardware shop. They also found another shop in Bootham, number 24, next to the Bootham Tavern. Most family members were involved in the business at some time or other, whether in the shops themselves or behind the scenes baking, making and icing cakes. The family decided to move the bakehouse from Burton Stone Lane to the rear of the Clifton shop, and this was built in 1957. Jack Dandy had sold his Nunnery Lane shop and did the baking himself. Number 22 Burton Stone Lane was converted into flats.

Pam Young knew the family.

Dick was lovely. He had four daughters. He was so funny. He would make a joke out of anything. He was a very handy person, could do anything with his hands. Betty, his wife, was lovely as well. She was

223

Dandy's van in 1950s (Marilyn Powell)

a very capable, sensible, down to earth woman who taught all her daughters to be self reliant. Obviously times weren't easy and she was a very determined woman was Hilda. She was the driving force, the matriarch. Sometimes Kathleen Mary used to tell me the stories [about] the war and the wedding cake. They couldn't afford to get all the ingredients, I presume they would use things like powdered egg, quite often the cake was in a hollow shell. There was a wedding one, they had the bottom one as cake, but it had pillars. But as she put this cake together, the whole thing sank into the first one. Socially the Dandys were 'up there'. Everybody would have known Dick and everybody would have liked him.

Kathleen Mary and Sid lived in St Peter's Grove. They had a big house there and two flats within the house. Hilda and Jack lived at Burton Stone Lane, and Hilda had bought up a lot of property in Clifton, and rented it out, [121-127 Clifton]. They're very big houses, not just three storeys but a cellar and an attic. Dick Dandy lived opposite the church. When the daughters got married, all they had to do was hold up the traffic and walk across, they never needed a wedding car.

The family also bought 9-11 Stonegate in 1954, and adjoining properties in Little Stonegate, renting them out at various times to the British School of Motoring, a hairdressing business, and later the Old World Club.

Dandy's in 1950s (Marilyn Powell)

The Yorkshire Evening Press reported that a limited company was formed in 1960, to take over 'the business of Hilda, Betty and D B Dandy, S and K Anderson, at Clifton, Bootham and Crichton Avenue'. This was the York Coffee House Company, and the directors were Arthur Rymer, Herbert Harrowell, George Cromlie, Arthur Gladwin and William Duff. Dick Dandy continued as manager for three years. The business ceased trading in 1967 and the premises were sold in 1971 to William Wright, butcher's, who had been trading next door at 53 Clifton, since the 1960s.

Local people remember Dandy's with affection, including Pauline Wright.

They had a warehouse at the top of Burton Stone Lane. I remember going up for cakes when we were having the Sunday school parties.

Lena Mills

knew Mrs Dandy, the old lady. They used to help us with catering at chapel. They were members of the church.

225

Boys at St Peter's School enjoyed going there, like Hugh Murray.

We'd go down there and buy Battenberg cake. That was before we had a tuck shop.

Dick Dandy remembers the school boys before the war, as

very good customers who visited the kiosk to purchase ices and sweets. The grandly named kiosk was a converted shed with a sliding window in the small front garden of 39 Compton Street. Mr Toyne was headmaster of the school and I remember mother being most upset when the kiosk was put out of bounds, diminishing our sales. On special cricket match fixtures, we were asked to provide ice cream for the school tuck shop, managed by a Mrs Roberts. It was my job to deliver the ices packed in a tub with ice and salt.

Dandy's also did outside catering including birthday parties and wedding receptions. Some took place in the Clifton Cinema ballroom.

Wedding reception of Eileen Race and RAF pilot Jack Wood at Clifton Cinema ballroom 1955 *(Eileen Race)*

Hilda Dandy would ice the wedding cakes and other wives and sisters would be involved. Marilyn Powell recalls being taken along to 'help' at these receptions as a young girl and being fascinated by the artistic ability of her grandmother.

CLIFTON CARRIAGEWORKS

Clifton Carriageworks made carriages for horses, and was situated where Clifton Cinema now stands. It was demolished, but there was another business of 'motor body builders' of the same name, in Avenue Road, off Burton Stone Lane, in the 1950s. The Yorkshire

Evening Press reported in February 1962 that Clifton Carriageworks was to have the use of the site in Avenue Road for vehicle parking. The coachbuilding firm was taken over by the Appleyard Group of Leeds in 1966 but was still open under the name of Clifton Carriageworks in the 1970s.

GARAGES

There were several garages in Clifton from the 1930s to the 1960s. Kitch's garage was a small establishment based in Barker's Yard, between 94 and 96 Clifton. Next to Willkins' newsagent, was the Lofthouse garage, owned by Tom Lofthouse and then his son Don. The garage did vehicle repairs for Dandy's bakery, who purchased their delivery vans from them. It eventually became Clifton Garage, which won an award in March 1985 from Renault UK for its customer service. The dealership with Renault ended in 1988. The garage has now been demolished.

Don Lofthouse at Lofthouse Garage 1930s (York Oral History Society)

Lofthouse Garage 1952 (York Oral History Society)

Clifton Green Garages, motor car agents and dealers at 122 Clifton, was run by Mr Loadman, husband of the headmistress of Ebor School, at 116 Clifton. There was also a showroom with cars on display. Part of the building became Jarman and Flint, grocers, in the 1960s, and by the end of the decade the garage had gone, to be replaced by Frank Dee grocers, (which had begun as Mrs Dee's grocery in a cottage closer to Highcliffe Court). Today this is the Spar supermarket.

NORTHERN PISTON SUPPLIES

Peter Willow's first job was

> *down Compton Street, at Northern Piston Supplies, it had been part of Bootham Engineers. I swept the floor, made tea and went out on the carrier bike. I went on to do stock cards, I knew all the jobs in the end. At first I used to deliver on a carrier bike round York. I had curly hair and they sent me for a mop head, the requisition said,*

'One mop head, as pattern', meaning my curly hair. I'd go all over York with this carrier bike, it was so heavy that when you loaded stuff in the basket at the front, the back wheel would come off the ground until I sat on it. It was hard to pedal. I was given a wet weather outfit like a seaman's outfit which I'd never wear. Fashion was coming in, in 1965! It was a sou-wester, a cape and some leggings. My job was also packing parcels and you'd put parcels on a bus. So if a garage in Easingwold wanted parts for a car, they'd ring up, order them and I'd take them to the bus stop. There were quite a few carrier bike boys putting different commodities on buses. You'd go to different bus stops, the station, Piccadilly, the Pullman office on Navigation Road.

I think my first wage was £2. 16s 8d for more than 40 hours a week. I once stopped that building getting burnt down. I'd been on duty with [someone called] *Don and he smoked a pipe and, just before we locked up, he emptied his pipe into a litter bin, a tea chest that we put the parcel wrappings into. I went back to check everything was off and I could smell burning, in the tea-chest. We ended up putting it out or we'd have locked up and the building would have burnt down. It was well on its way! I think we cleaned it up and kept it quiet. There were some real characters, with Don, and Bill who'd been a policeman in Garforth and used to tell me stories. All the characters who'd been through World War Two were interesting people, they'd been through so much. It was taken over by successive companies, Associated Engineering and Edmunds Walker.*

– Chapter 14 –
LEISURE AND ENTERTAINMENT

Before the advent of television and computer games, people made their own entertainment. The upper classes had balls, bridge evenings and musical soirees. For working people, there were small clubs and societies, often based in public houses. Clifton was no exception. As well as the Burton Stone Lane Adult School Social Club which opened in 1905, there were also two working men's clubs, a Floral and Horticultural Society formed in 1879, Darby and Joan Club, an Allotment Holders Association, and several sports clubs.

Bert Keech at his Bowling Club 1940s
(York Oral History Society)

BOWLING

Sheila Goater recalls the Bert Keech bowling club in Sycamore Terrace, formerly Bootham Bowling Club. The Keech Club was formed in 1949, with its first annual dinner in 1956.

He started this more or less as a private bowling club. Somewhere along there, a Roman burial was found and a ladies' comb which suggested it was a Christian burial. Before the Bert Keech Club it was a tennis club. Then he bought the ground and two great big houses next to it.

My father belonged to the club, my mother joined when we all left home. Father used to play bowls every summer night. Bert Keech himself also had the lease of the De Grey Rooms and they had dances. I met my husband there.

Clifton Bowling Club was formed in 1902, the green being in Grove View and the headquarters at the Old Grey Mare. The pavilion was an old railway carriage. One of its members was Bob Jennings, a noted football league referee between the wars.

Clifton Bowling Club (Joan Aherne)

The club regularly held 'smoking concerts' during the winter time, when members gathered in the Old Grey Mare and smoked tobacco in clay pipes. There was a programme of songs and recitations, and the tall stories got taller as the ale flowed. The club was a private one with shareholder members. It went into voluntary liquidation in April 1959, and the land was sold to St Peter's School.

CLIFTON PARK

The new Clifton Park Clubhouse opened in April 2010 though the Park has been home to cricket, rugby union, rugby league, tennis and squash for over 40 years. Clifton Cricket Club was formed in 1784, three years before the MCC. It moved to Bootham Crescent in 1881, to Wigginton Road in 1932 and Clifton Park on Shipton Road in 1967, along with York Rugby Union Club.

John Linfoot has been

Chairman of York Tennis Club for the last 25 years. In 1966, Tang Hall Tennis Club, which I was a member of, were losing our premises in the grounds of Tang Hall Hotel. The brewery wanted more of the land so they gave us notice to quit, which coincided with a club called Sycamore, who played in Water Lane on the site of the YWCA, opposite the doctor's surgery, also having to move. We joined them to play on the courts in Water Lane as Clifton Tennis Club. The following year we moved to Clifton Park, playing on three shale courts. We now have six courts, five are astro turf and one is a carpet court. Ladies hockey was there for quite a while, and also an archery club, but they've been gone some years.

[In tennis], we've got 16 competitive sides in various leagues. There's a local ladies league, we have two teams in that, a local mens' doubles league, we have four teams in that and a national league team. But we welcome new members. We've got a flourishing junior section of about 100 members, ranging from five or six up to 16. We've got a flourishing day membership of housewives and retirees who come down, the whole gamut of ages right through. Because the surface is so user friendly, it is artificial grass, people are playing well into their 70s.

We have a full time coach attached to the club, Bev Cairns, and we're just about to get a performance coach. One of my roles is to distribute Wimbledon tickets to all the clubs in the York area who are affiliated to the York LTA [Lawn Tennis Association]. *It's a long day from York but a lot of people do go. There's always an upsurge in tennis around that time. I am a qualified elementary coach but I don't coach much now. The LTA are working very hard to promote tennis at grass roots level. We've got a winter league with floodlights. You can play under any conditions apart from snow.*

FOOTBALL

The first York City Football Club (at that time amateur) was in Holgate. In 1912 the club acquired a plot of land known as Field View off Burton Stone Lane, then went to Fulford, before moving to Bootham Crescent in the 1930s, where it remains today. The team got to the semi finals of the FA Cup in 1955 and once reached the second division in 1974-6. In the 1930s crowds averaged 4,000, but it was in the late 1940s, when men were returning from the war, that the game was at its peak and was the major form of entertainment (with predominantly male spectators) in the city. Crowds often reached 8,000 on Saturday afternoons.

ROLLER SKATING

Roller skating was hugely popular in the period before the First World War, and there were several rinks in York, including one in Sycamore Terrace. There were lots of competitions in the skating league against other clubs.

CLIFTON CYCLING CLUB

Clifton Cycling Club was founded in 1895 and held its meetings at the Grey Mare. In the first winter, the river was frozen and two men rode from York to Poppleton on the ice on their tandem. Over the ensuing years, there were many competitions, with trophies being presented annually at the club dinner. Women were only able to join the club in 1923. Members went on to take part in more serious events and races, including time trialling, hill climbing, and even participated in the world championships.

Clifton Cycling Club 1906 (*York Oral History Society*)

Clifton Cycling Club event 2010 (*Christine Kyriacou*)

More about football, cycling, tennis and other sports will be covered in my next book, on Sport in York (2012).

PIGEON RACING

Malcolm Maher began to race pigeons from a young age.

I was born in 1937 at 84 Spalding Avenue. I had pigeons because my dad helped us. I had an interest, it increased in 1968 when a young grizzle hen dropped into my garden, flown out and in need of assistance. I looked after it for some time before it was well enough to be reported. It was the property of Alf Chorley of Kendal, and it was sent back. It returned to me at Christmas and so was transferred to me. This was the start of my racing pigeons. I obtained a few others from local fanciers and started racing. The grizzle hen scored for me [over the next few years]. *I formed a close friendship with Billie Little. I obtained birds from him each year and started racing the youngsters he bred for me in 1969. You used to train them three times a week.*

Malcolm Maher on left 1950s
(*Malcolm Maher*)

In the Imperial, you'd go Friday night and basket them. They set the clocks, for say seven o'clock at night and then sealed them. Everybody would have their birds there and you had a rubber ring with the number on, you put it round the bird's leg and it clicked on. Then they went into special crates, onto a transporter. The farthest they'd go would be down to t'coast [south coast, to go over the Channel]. *They let you know the next day what time the pigeons are liberated, so then you're waiting. Somebody that liberated it knew all about the weather. You had a committee of them doing it.* [Checking the time of each bird]. *Some was really fairly close sometimes.*

One of Malcolm's best pigeons was the Imperial Sovereign, which won cups and prizes including one for the Bourges race in June 1976. Malcolm was the highest prize winner in the Imperial Club which had about 50 members in 1975, and became president of the Imperial Pigeon Club for two years. He had prizes for birds which flew to,

Malcolm Maher (in centre) wins cups for pigeon racing (Malcolm Maher)

Montlucon 553 miles, Melun 410 miles, Lewes about 220 miles and others inland. The bird that topped the Yorkshire Middle Route federation from Bourges was from the no. 5 cock and no. 1 hen of Billie Little. He was released with the rest of the convoy at 6am and I clocked him at 7.23pm being just over 13 hours for 502 miles fly. He scored a first as a young bird.

There's a man called Dr Shiow in Taiwan, he came and bought them.

Imperial Sovereign
NU 72H 1253

Owned by MALCOLM MAHER
Imperial Homing Society YORK
1st Club — 1st Western Section
1st Yorks. Middle Route Federation
Bourges Race 25th June, 1976
2,827 Birds Velocity 1098 y.p.m.
501 Miles, 1163 Yds.

Imperial Sovereign, pigeon raced by
Malcolm Maher 1976
(Malcolm Maher)

I sent him the first lot, took them to Heathrow Airport. He flew from Paris over to England and I picked him up at York station and he stayed here one night. He offered me 2000 dollars for Imperial Sovereign, but I never sold it. Two years later I put an extension on and the birds didn't go out for six weeks. Then I let the birds out and I've never seen it since. When they closed the Imperial, we moved [the club] to Clifton Hotel.

PUBLIC HOUSES

As well as the pubs in Burton Stone Lane, there were several pubs in Clifton. The Mitre on Shipton Road which opened in 1961, The Clifton Hotel on Kingsway, first mentioned in the 1930s, the Bumper Castle in Wigginton Road on the edge of the aerodrome, and the Old Grey Mare near Clifton Green, all still exist. The Grey Mare is a 17th century coaching inn. In 1820 it was known as the Grey Horse and by the 1950s became Ye Olde Grey Mare and is now the Old Grey Mare. The Maypole near Clifton Green may have been a predecessor. Hugh Murray records that, 'In 1647 Helen and Elizabeth Drysdale were executed at St Leonard's Gallows for wilfully and deliberately poisoning with oxalic acid two young men who were paying their addresses to them there'.

The Bumper Castle on Wigginton Road was built in 1846 for William Johnson. His widow continued the business until she died at the age of 102 in 1907, the oldest licence holder in Britain.

Margaret Arnold lived there during the war.

At weekends everybody walked along Wigginton Road to Bumper

Old Grey Mare trip 1936. Robert Lacy fifth from right at back. Ernest Inns (father of Margaret Arnold) 2nd from left kneeling. Georgie Plummer is smallest man standing. Seventh from right at back is Patrick Aherne, Joan Aherne's father in law (Margaret Arnold)

Castle especially Saturday and Sunday nights. We had a big garden and my father had built swings and a seesaw. He also did a nine hole putting green. I used to like doing that. When I was learning to do handstands, I remember my mother saying I spent more time upside down than the right way. Bumper Castle had a bar, a smoke room and a lounge, two other small rooms. In the lounge we had an air raid shelter.

Doug Heald liked the Bumper Castle

It was a place of entertainment. In the early '60s they had this list of all the Coronation Street characters who had been in. It would be a meeting place and there'd be someone singing, Audrey Stead on the drums and Mick on the piano. Tommy Stead was the one who owned it. He said he'd been on the Palladium and he'd get up and

Bumper Castle 2011 (Christine Kyriacou)

give a Maurice Chevalier. It was always a good atmosphere. It's all disappeared, pubs are not the same.

The Sycamore on Water End was known as the Green Tree in 1825 and the Sycamore Tree in 1838. It closed as an inn many years ago.

Lucy Staples lives nearby.

It's called the White House, a private house now. It had a paddock but several years ago that was sold off. It has a reasonable sized garden, very nice.

The Imperial on Crichton Avenue opened in 1937, but closed down and was demolished in 1994.

Imperial, Crichton Avenue (Hugh Murray)

Doug Heald recalls,

> *It was a very big pub, a notorious pub, it was nicknamed the Stalingrad. It was a working pub. They had the allotments* [near there] *and people keeping pigs and hens and ponies.*

Malcolm Maher played rugby

> *for the Imperial, on the back fields, where the prisoner of war camp was. We went from there up onto Wiggy Road, on the Stray. Before that I played for Clifton Hotel. It would be about 1959. Then they got into the top rugby league.*

YOUTH CLUBS

Clifton Recreation Youth Club opened in May 1942. Gill May recalls the youth club in the church hall, Water Lane.

Imperial rugby team. Malcolm Maher far right at front. 1959 (Malcolm Maher)

I'd have been 15. Next to the church there was a little school. We had the youth club there when I first started going. I remember more about the bigger church hall in Water Lane.

On Friday night they had dances, and ballroom dancing. We all danced away to the Beatles. The family who lived next door to the vicarage, Mr Hardy, his son went to the youth club, and he actually came and helped. He got us all doing a pantomime.

They started up a netball tournament. That was one of the things I really did like. It was more fun.

YORK BURTON LANE CLUB AND INSTITUTE

This working men's club was formed in 1900, initially in a house in Ratcliffe Street, Burton Stone Lane. It moved round the corner to an old joiner's workshop in Bootham Crescent, with a loan of £1200 from John Smith's brewery. Major extensions took place in 1930. Wives were only allowed to come along to the outings to the seaside or to help with the annual harvest festival and flower show, when hymns were sung before the auctioning of the produce. A library of books and newspapers also provided technical books to help members with their apprenticeships.

Burton Lane Club outing 1900s

Other facilities included a club bath, a bowling green at the front of the club, with games such as billiards, snooker, darts, dominoes, whist, cribbage, angling, cricket, cycling and brasses. There was also a male voice choir. The club still exists.

YORK GALA

Asylum Field on Bootham Park near Bootham Hospital, was the site of the Grand Yorkshire Gala, later the York Gala. Each June, from 1858, the three day festival was visited by residents of York and way beyond. The record attendance was 57,383 in 1899. Excursion trains from Yorkshire, Northumberland and Durham, Lancashire, Lincolnshire and even London poured into the city.

One of the objects of the Gala was to raise money for York charities such as the County Hospital and the soup kitchens in the city. There was plenty of entertainment with various stalls, and military bands. Signor Beneditti with his sword swallowing act, and Professor Heriot and his daughter Louie with their magic act, were familiar sights. Large marquees for exhibiting flowers and fruit were provided. Nurseries from all over the country exhibited there. All kinds of fruit were represented, including peaches, grapes and nectarines. Fuchsias, exotic ferns, pelargoniums, alpines, azaleas, roses and orchids were a key feature. It was felt by many that the Royal Horticultural Society ought to hold its annual flower show in York instead of Chelsea. In the evenings, music for dancing was provided and the event would end with fireworks.

York Gala 1900s (*York Oral History Society*)

But the highlight was the hot air balloon. The first balloon flight in York, in June 1859, featured balloonist Henry Coxwell, who flew in from Derby. He described the event for the local press.

> *There was a massive crowd which became unsteady as the day wore on. Mr Tom Smith, a local worthy, assisted as some of the crowd tried to release the balloon. One man yelled 'Let go'* [of the guy ropes] *so I punched him on the nose. We set off but it was low, and it just missed the refreshment hut. We cut through the trees with the lower part of the balloon, crouched down, and got clear. We landed safely.*

In 1893, one of the hottest summers on record, the Yorkshire Evening Press reported glorious weather and excellent crowds, and 'the mysterious, weird and soul-creeping séance' held in a tent. 52,915 people attended. That year a York schoolboy, Walter Way, was dying from a brain tumour but, when his sister visited him, he expressed a desire to go to the Gala which he enjoyed. But he became increasingly ill and had to be rushed back to the Industrial School where he died. His body was escorted to St Mary's Church, Castlegate, by friends from school, and the church was packed with his friends and teachers.

Ethel Thomson recorded her visits in her book 'Clifton Lodge'.

> *Every June we visited the gala. One year we made an ascent in a captive balloon. There were usually two balloons, one a captive tied to a steel cable operated by a traction engine, and the other the 'right away' which soared aloft with Captain Spencer in command. If you wanted to accompany him you had to pay £5, but for five shillings you could have a trip in a captive balloon and be taken to a height of 500 feet. What captivated me was the variety of entertainment on a stage on one side of the field. Trick bicyclists, trapeze artists, performing dogs, clowns, singers of comic or sentimental songs, aroused my keenest enthusiasm.*

Hot air balloon at Gala (York Oral History Society)

In 1911 a tragi-comic event occurred.

The Board of Trade regulations provided that a servant of the company must accompany each ascent. Messrs Spencer sent a boy up who had no knowledge of ballooning. The balloon also contained a deaf and dumb man, an acrobat belonging to one of the variety troupes, and a woman who has no claim to fame beyond the fact that she was wearing her best hat. On arrival at the 500 feet limit, the rope suddenly broke and the balloon changed from 'captive' to 'right away' and to the horror of the passengers and spectators, went sailing away into the blue heaven. None of the occupants had the faintest idea what to do and the balloon continued to rise higher and higher. The nose of the woman wearing her best hat began to bleed and she was crying. This put heroism into the heart of the acrobat, and he climbed up the network of ropes and made a gash in the side of the balloon with his pocket knife. Gradually gas began to escape and after a little time a descent began. When they bumped into the

*first tree the woman thought they would be mangled to death, and
in order to save her hat from destruction she threw it out into a
ploughed field. The acrobat thought that if he were to jump out he
might be able to catch hold of the trailing rope and draw the balloon
gently to earth. So he turned a series of somersaults, landed safely
on terra firma and looked round for the rope, when lo and behold,
he saw the balloon, on losing his weight, leap up above the trees and
being carried by the wind across the fields much faster than he could
have imagined possible.*

*By this time people in motor cars had come out from York and were
following the balloon, and a crowd of bicyclists also joined in pursuit.
After being caught up again in a few trees and hedges, and being
bumped about unmercifully, the party was rescued and all drove
back to the gala field, where a rousing reception awaited them. The
acrobat was due on the variety stage to do his 'turn', the woman
was too faint to say a word, the boy was being interviewed by his
employers, there only remained the deaf and dumb man to cope with
the excited, questioning crowd. A reporter hurled questions at him
to no avail. Not to be outdone, he handed the man a notebook and
pencil, hoping to gain an exclusive. The man thought deeply for a few
moments and then began to write. When he handed his message over,
it read 'The rope broke' which, after all, explained the event perfectly.*

In the 1920s, the show moved to the Knavesmire where entry fees and
car park charges could boost finances. Unfortunately by 1931, the Gala,
after three bad summers and the Depression, was losing money and it was
decided to abandon it, which was felt to be a great loss to York.

CLIFTON CINEMA/BINGO CLUB

Clifton Cinema opened on 17th November 1937, the last cinema of its
kind to be built in the city, on the site of Clifton Carriageworks, motor
body builders. The building and its interior were designed by Frederick
Dyer in the Art Deco style, and owned by JX (Jack) Prendergast who also
owned the Rialto (now Mecca) on Fishergate, and other cinemas outside

York and was an entrepreneur in the city, responsible for bringing world famous artists to concerts there. For the opening night, a welcome was extended to the public 'and particularly to the inhabitants of Clifton and district'. The cinema had accommodation for 750 in the stalls and 390 in the balcony, the latter including some 'double courting seats', and had two foyers, on the ground and first floor. The foyer had a paybox in the centre, in which the cashier was locked. Films were shown continually each day from 2pm to 10.30, so it was possible to see a film two or three times.

CLIFTON CINEMA YORK

ATTRACTIONS FOR
MARCH - - 1938

Clifton Cinema programme 1938
(York Oral History Society)

Jeremy Prendergast, grandson of JX, explains,

It was opened by Michael Powell. At that time he would have been a very young director and he'd made a film called 'The Edge of the World', a drama documentary. My grandfather invited him to attend the opening, - he made a speech and the film was shown.

My grandfather formed an association with Mr Mawson who owned what used to be Barclays Bank next door. On our deeds it shows that the cinema is built in the garden of that house. It was like rose gardens, formal gardens.

The opening night programme stated that 'the seats are designed for real comfort – into which one will sink with a sigh of relief…By means of the latest scientific equipment the air supply to the theatre is cleansed, washed and tempered to the needs of the season'. Mr Prendergast's 'endeavour will be to amuse, to thrill, to enchant, to foster human sympathies, to cater for the music lover, the 'highbrow' and the 'lowbrow', and to leave all its patrons with a feeling that the evening has not been wasted but has been a time of joy and refreshment'. The cinema was equipped with a Compton organ, first played in 1938, but removed in the early 1960s. In 1939 an air raid siren was placed on the roof of the building. After the war it was tested and maintained annually by a man from the Ministry of Defence. When the Berlin wall came down in 1989, and the threat of nuclear war seemed more remote, the siren was taken away. Wartime was a busy time for the cinema. The Pathe newsreels usually preceded the main film and gave the public the opportunity to find out what was happening in the world. Cinema was also a necessary means of escape, with Fred Astaire and Ginger Rogers' musicals proving very popular. Films were sometimes shared between several cinemas, and taken round the town by a courier on a bicycle.

RIALTO CLIFTON

Where FISHERGATE Is —Telephone 3680—

THREE DAYS ONLY.	THREE DAYS.
ERROL FLYNN, CLAUDE RAINS, ALLAN HALE, FLORA ROBSON, BRENDA MARSHALL.	**Errol Flynn, Paul Lukas,**
IN	—— in ——
" THE SEA HAWK "	**" Uncertain Glory "**
The Screen's Greatest Romantic Spectacle.	At 1.45, 3.45, 5.50, 8.15.
App. at 1.40, 3.52, 6.9, 8.31.	Comedy at 3.20, 5.25, 7.50.
And Full Programme.	NEWS: at 3.35, 5.40, 8.5.
NEWS approx. 3.42, 5.59, 8.21.	Edward Farley at the Organ, 7.30.
Edward Farley at the Organ: 8.11.	And Full Programme.

Clifton Cinema 1945 (The Press)

The cinema had a ballroom on the first floor, which was used for dances and also hired out for parties and wedding receptions. Tony Lister managed the cinema and ballroom from 1938 to the 1950s. He was master of ceremonies at the Rialto and, in 1934, Jack Prendergast sent him for training with world ballroom champions Maxwell Stuart and Pat Sykes. In November 1953, the Yorkshire Evening Press announced

Clifton ballroom practice class tonight
8-10pm. 1s 6d under the direction of Tony Lister, MISTD, MIDMA

By the late 1950s, ballroom dancing was becoming less popular as other forms of entertainment came along. The York Jazz Club used the ballroom for a few years. The Yorkshire Evening Press of 7th December 1960 advertised

York Jazz Club, above Clifton Cinema, tonight
Burgundy Jazz Club. 8pm to 11pm. 2s 6d

Doug Heald went to the

jazz club on a Thursday night, while I was at York School of Art. It

Dance 1962 at Clifton Cinema ballroom, Neal Guppy facing in centre (Neal Guppy)

would be trad jazz. They had live bands. You had the beatniks, the more serious types, at the Art School, and the modern way of dress, the rock and roll days, tight drainpipes, black shirts. You'd have these contrasts.

Neal Guppy, who later founded the Enterprise Club, held record parties and jive classes in the ballroom from 1961, attracting as many as 200 young people. In March 1963 he hosted a 'Wild West fancy dress night from 8 to 11pm, with tickets at 3/6d'. In May the ballroom held another fancy dress evening, 'Jiving to the Morvans [the group managed by Neal] and all the latest pops'.

In 1963, the cinema became a cine-bingo club, showing films for three days of the week, and offering bingo for four nights. There were also Saturday afternoon children's matinees. In January 1964, it announced,

CLIFTON BINGO AND SOCIAL CLUB YORK

WEDNESDAY AFTERNOON, FEBRUARY 14th

DOORS OPEN 1.30   **EYES DOWN 2.30**

18 GAMES OF BINGO
☞ **ADMISSION 1/6** ☜

PRIZE MONEY
WILL BE OVER
£300!

Clifton Bingo and Social Club 1968 (The Press)

Cine Bingo Club. Every Thursday, Friday, Saturday and Sunday.
Eyes down 7.30. £300 golden scoop. House jackpot £100.
Car park for 200 cabs at rear of cinema.

Mr Prendergast's love of films is something which has spread right through the family. His son was the famous film composer, John Barry, whose rock and roll group the John Barry Seven rehearsed at Clifton in the 1950s and who died in 2011. His other son Patrick was involved in the running of Clifton Cinema, and sometimes projected the films.

Patrick Prendergast (Jonathan Prendergast)

Patrick's two sons, Jonathan and Jeremy Prendergast, eventually came into the business. Jonathan is now Chairman of the company, and Jeremy the Managing Director. Jeremy explains,

My father was very involved in the cinema period. He used to do a lot of the film booking and the publicity material. He then managed the

John Barry and Jonathan Prendergast at Clifton Bingo Club 1987 (Jonathan Prendergast)

bingo club, but I'd have to say he was very much a cinema person and I think he was quite unhappy at the change-over. Cinema owners had these buildings and they weren't really quite sure the way business was going to develop, so different forms of entertainment were tried out. Cinema in the '20s and '30s was very much tied in with dancing and ballroom, I think he [JX] loved the idea of variety entertainment, cinema mixing with ballroom, with music, with comedians and entertainers.

For several years in the 1960s, the cinema also had its own casino. Jack Senescal, who had worked in management services for British Rail, was brought in to help run it.

In '68 the Gaming Act came in, which outlawed small casinos. I think the worry was that it could be used as a criminal thing, a way of laundering money. But it was all small stakes gaming, I think the maximum stake was half a crown. [They played] *roulette, crown*

Casino at Clifton Cinema. 1960s (Jeremy Prendergast)

and anchor which is a dice game, and I think card games. I know of customers that remember it and were sad it had to come to an end. It was very much my father's little enterprise.

By the mid 1960s, the advent of television in almost every home had a huge effect on cinema-going and the cinema side closed down completely, the company becoming Clifton Bingo and Social Club. The main auditorium still has a cinema feel to it, with steps down from the balcony area to a big stage with satin curtains. Jeremy describes the changes,

Through to the '70s, '80s, when you walked in, it would feel like a cinema building, with cinema seats and a raised floor. There was a very big refurbishment in the mid '80s which went from cinema seats to unit seating, a fixed table with four seats. Since then we've just revised that, improved the layout, the equipment, the décor. Coloured glass was a very '30s thing. The thinking behind the colour scheme, it was those warm '30s colours. We copied an original grille design from the vents in the main hall, something that was original to a 1930s building and taken that as a bit of a motif. The carpet was inspired by a Gustav Klimt design. But the light fittings, everything, there's a definite 1930s reference. The building has [still] got an atmosphere.

Jeremy and Jonathan Prendergast in projection room at Clifton Bingo Club 1980s
(The Press)

Jonathan Prendergast was born in 1954, and began working at Clifton Bingo in the evenings whilst doing a two year foundation course at York Art School, after St Peter's School. Although he had a place at university, his father asked him to go into the business and he agreed, making it his career.

My grandfather owned several cinemas and co-owned the Astoria in Hull, which was the biggest outside the Clifton. He also owned a company, True-Vue Ltd, in the grounds of Fulford House, with Patrick and his son in law David Lloyd-Jones. They made and installed cinema screens. They used a silver paint which, when sprayed on the screen, did not reflect. It used a secret formula. They also later did stage set-ups for bingo clubs. When the company liquidated, some of the lads there went on to work at Saville's Audio Visual. My father, Patrick, was asked if he wanted to manage the Mecca when the Rialto was sold, but declined and for a while worked for True-Vue.

In the early days, when I first worked full time at the Clifton, my two younger sisters, Joanna and Jessica, used to work there part time for pocket money, mainly on the coffee bar. My wife also helped then and some of my children also worked there. Famously, my uncle (and godfather) John Barry worked in the projection room at the Rialto and June, his sister, also worked in the business. Even my grandmother, Doris, had run the sweet shop outside the Rialto and was responsible for that aspect at the Clifton in the cinema days.

When I started at 18, my grandfather was still active in the executive decision-making and I had to discuss any changes with him to get them agreed. I had to ring him at the end of every evening session with the day's takings, which I read in code. I worked for him for seven years before he died in December 1978. Obviously I was also still working with my father who was happy to take more of a background role.

I started just when decimalization came in, selling tote tickets (any two numbers between 1-30), which were very popular but since made illegal. Working every aspect of the business was good grounding. It's interesting to note that studies have shown that playing bingo keeps players' minds younger for longer! Rapid hand-eye coordination is used to scan the bingo cards. Players have a bigger chance of maintaining their mental alertness.

I started calling on prize bingo at the front of the stage in the '70s with 75-numbered American bingo. Then I called main stage bingo, the traditional 90-numbered game for much larger money prizes. It was the customer's money we were playing with and it was a serious job. Calling was really enjoyable. We weren't allowed to use any of the colloquial terminology as the gaming board had outlawed its use before I started calling. [Such phrases as 'Two little ducks, – 22, quack, quack'.]

Clifton Bingo Club 2011 (Van Wilson)

With regards to the caller's stage console, originally we had a bingo 'blower', with balls blown by a fan motor up a tube, which stopped at the top ready to be pulled out. We would ask a player-witness to sit at the side of the caller who would show them each ball as it came out before placing it in the top tray. Then we replaced the witness on stage with a camera at the top of the tube, and the balls were shown on monitors around the hall. The checker would take the winning ticket to a camera point (a box with mirror at 45° and a camera) so that the customers could see the marked numbers on the screens. Then the Random Number Generators started being used. They are very quiet and efficient but lack a bit of fun the bingo blowers had.

We once had a woman caller who got an electric shock trying to release a ball stuck in the tray with her finger whilst calling and she fainted. After that, every bingo blower in the UK had to be fitted with plastic cable trunking to cover the micro-switches underneath (that triggered a display board) for health and safety.

Wall art outside Clifton Bingo Club, painted by Keith Hopewell, friend of the Prendergasts
(Van Wilson)

Today Clifton Bingo Club still has the cinema's original projection room, with two projectors, Peerless high intensity lamps and a cupboard with rectifiers looking 'like something out of Frankenstein'. There is also a rewinding room where the films were rewound before being returned. The room is now used for storage. The club is still an important part of the community, as Jeremy explains,

We're a social form of gaming, people come here primarily to meet friends and to enjoy nights out. It's a community thing. People tell you that it really does mean a lot to them. It's one of the

environments where you get age groups mixing. On the whole, things are quite polarised these days but with bingo, that isn't the case. Grand-daughters will come out with grandmothers. Commercial bingo has always been professionally run and controlled legally. There's people playing books, and during the intervals playing cash bingo. We also have electronic bingo which allows people to play extra sets of books, they don't have to keep up with the numbers, they just press the button and that catches up with what the caller calls. We've got five or six people who can call. We have a bar and a catering operation as well. On a busy night you can have 3 or 400 people in here, it has a good atmosphere.

He feels that his grandfather's legacy is still there.

Certainly you felt his presence and continue to do so. He had an extraordinary life really. I hugely admire and respect what he did.

Clifton Bingo and Social Club 1992 (Van Wilson)

EPILOGUE

Clifton's transition from rural area to village to sprawling suburb has happened gradually. The farmers and agricultural labourers of the 17th and 18th centuries would be astonished at the development which has taken place. The widening of the city boundaries means that most of Clifton is now part of the city of York. The A19, once the turnpike road to Easingwold, is built up with housing estates, sports clubs and large hotels. Clifton, still with its village-like charm, flows seamlessly into Rawcliffe and Skelton, yet is still close to York city centre.

This is the story of Clifton's expansion, an area well-loved by its inhabitants, so many of whom were born and remain there, with the voices of some of those who have taken part in its development. It is dedicated to all Cliftonites past and present.

BIBLIOGRAPHY

BENSON, George. *York*. Blackie & Son, 1911

BRINKLOW, D. (Ed.) *Lumley Barracks, Burton Stone Lane, York. Report on an Archaeological Desk-top Study*. York Archaeological Trust, 2001

CANON LEE SCHOOL. *Canon Lee 1941-1991*. Canon Lee School, 1991

DEPARTMENT OF HEALTH. *The Kerr/Haslam Inquiry*. July 2005

HUTTON, Barbara. *Clifton and its People in the 19th Century*. York Philosophical Society, 1969

KANER, Jennifer. *'Clifton and Medieval Woolhouses'* in York Historian 8, 1988. York Architectural and Yorkshire Archaeological Society, 1988

KNIGHT, C. B. *A History of the City of York*. Herald Printing Works, 1944

MURRAY, Hugh. *A Directory of York Pubs 1455-2004*. Voyager Publications, 2004.

NEWMAN, Mona. *The Parish Church of St Philip and St James, Clifton 1867-1967*. Published by the church, 1967

PAGE, Stan. *A Very Short History of Clifton Hospital*. Privately published.

ROYAL COMMISSION ON HISTORICAL MONUMENTS. *City of York Vol. IV Outside the City Walls*. RCHM, 1975

ST PETER'S SCHOOL. *Prospectus 1980*. St Peter's School, 1980

SPENCE, Norman with Guy Jefferson and Ian Robinson. *The Airport that Never Was – The Story of Clifton Airfield*. Yorkshire Air Museum, 1999

THOMSON, Ethel, Lady. *Clifton Lodge*. Hutchinson, 1955

TILLOTT, P M (Ed.) *Victoria History of Counties of England. A History of Yorkshire: City of York.* Institute of Historical Research. Oxford University Press, 1961

WEBB, K.A. *From County Hospital to NHS Trust.* Borthwick Institute of Historical Research, 2002

YORK BURTON LANE CLUB AND INSTITUTE. *York Burton Lane Club and Institute 1900-1975.* York Burton Lane Club and Institute, 1975

Clifton Holme Annual Reports 1907-1936

Kelly's and White's Street Directories 1850s onwards

Plan of Burton Grange Estate 1910

Plan of Clifton Lodge Estates 1926 (Barry Parker of Letchworth)

Plan of Cliff Villa, Water End 1899

Records of the Homestead. Joseph Rowntree Foundation.

York Absent Voters' List 1918

York Census 1851, 1861

York Electoral Rolls

Yorkshire Evening Press (now The Press)

Yorkshire Gazette

www.britishlistedbuildings.co.uk

BBC History website

PUBLICATIONS BY THE SAME AUTHOR

The History of a Community : Fulford Road District of York.
University College of Ripon and York St John, 1984. Reprinted 1985

Alexina: A Woman in Wartime York. Voyager Publications, 1995

Rich in all but Money: Life in Hungate 1900-1938. York Archaeological
Trust, 1996. (Revised edition 2007)

Beyond the Postern Gate : A History of Fishergate and Fulford Road.
York Archaeological Trust, 1996

Humour, Heartache and Hope : Life in Walmgate.
York Archaeological Trust, 1996

York Voices. Tempus Publishing, 1999

Number 26 : The History of 26 St Saviourgate. Voyager Publications, 1999

Voices of St Paul's : An Oral History of St Paul's Church. (Edited)
William Sessions, 2001

*Rhythm and Romance : An Oral History of Popular Music in York. Volume 1 :
The Dance Band Years.* York Oral History Society, 2002

*Something in the Air : An Oral History of Popular Music in York. Volume 2 :
The Beat Goes On.* York Oral History Society, 2002

Rhythm and Romance : CD of The York Dance Band Era.
York Oral History Society, 2003

The Walmgate Story. Voyager Publications, 2006. Reprinted 2009

Something in the Air : CD of York Music in 1960s.
York Oral History Society, 2006

Rations, Raids and Romance : York in the Second World War.
York Archaeological Trust, 2008

Stonegate Voices. York Archaeological Trust, 2009

The Story of Terry's. York Oral History Society, 2009

The Best Years of Our Lives : Secondary Education in York 1900-1985.
York Archaeological Trust, 2010